# HIDDEN HEROES 6

# LIVING WATER IN THE DESERT

## True Stories of God at Work
## in Iran

I0897090

HIDDEN HEROES 6

# LIVING WATER IN THE DESERT

True Stories of God at Work

in Iran

# REBECCA DAVIS

CF4•K

10 9 8 7 6 5 4 3 2
Copyright © 2015 Rebecca Davis
ISBN: 978-1-78191-563-9

Published in 2015 and reprinted in 2016
by
Christian Focus Publications,
Geanies House, Fearn, Tain,
Ross-shire, IV20 1TW,
Great Britain

Cover design by Daniel van Straaten
Cover illustration by Jeff Anderson
Other illustrations by Jeff Anderson
Printed and bound by Nørhaven, Denmark

To the families of Haik Hovsepian and Hossein Soodmand and other martyrs, who continue to proclaim Jesus, knowing the cost.

To access more information and activities, see the *Living Water in the Desert* page at the Christian Focus website at www.christianfocus.com.

# Contents

1.  A HARD, DRY LAND ...............................................9

2.  KURDS AND THE WAY (SAEED) .................................11

3.  WILD WOMAN IN THE DESERT (MARY BIRD) ....... 19

4.  THE ONLY PROPHET THAT'S TRUE (RAJAB) ..... 25

5.  SOWING SEED IN A DESERT PLACE

    (WILLIAM MILLER) ........................................33

6.  STONE THE VICTORIOUS ONE (HASAN) ............39

7.  CHRISTIAN DOGS (HOSSEIN, PART ONE) ........... 47

8.  ARISE AND EAT! (HOSSEIN, PART TWO) ................ 55

9.  THE MYSTERIOUS BOOK (MINA, PART ONE)    63

10. WHO IS THAT YOUNG MAN?

    (MINA, PART TWO).....................................71

11. THE RELUCTANT SOLDIER (JAVID, PART ONE)    79

12. SOODMAND THE SHADOW

    (JAVID, PART TWO).........................................87

13. BLOOD OF THE MARTYRS, SEED OF

    THE CHURCH (HAIK, RASHIN) .............................95

14. THE IMAM WORSHIPER

    (PADINA, PART ONE) ...................................103

15. IRAN ALIVE! (PADINA, PART TWO) .........................111

16. A MAN ON A DONKEY (TAHER)...............................119

17. LIVING WATER IN THE DESERT ...........................127

A MESSAGE FROM THE AUTHOR .......................................129

ABOUT THE MISSIONARIES AND THE

    IRANIAN CHRISTIANS ........................................131

THINKING FURTHER .................................................135

# 1. A HARD, DRY LAND

In 1811, a young man named Henry Martyn arrived in Tehran, Persia with a very special gift for the Shah, the Muslim king of the land. It was the New Testament, translated into the Persian language for the first time ever.

But the Shah refused to see Henry Martyn. He wanted nothing to do with that book from a different religion.

Henry sadly went on his way, leaving the translation in another city. Shortly after this he died, only thirty-one years old.

Another man took the translation and printed many copies of it to sell or give away.

Another man translated the Old Testament into the Persian language.

A few missionaries came in those early years to the eight million people of Persia (which is now called Iran). But, at first, not many of those missionaries tried to reach the Muslim people for Christ. Those Muslims seemed so ... uninterested. So set in their ways. So hard-hearted.

Instead, most of the missionaries worked with the Assyrians and Armenians who lived in Persia—those groups of people had believed the Bible for centuries. Many of them became stronger in their faith, and they followed the examples of the missionaries.

And a few more missionaries came from the West. Only few Muslims came to Christ.

Persia ... Iran ... it was a hard, dry land.

The people were dying of thirst, needing the Living Water.

Over the next two hundred years, the Living Water sprinkled ... and then poured ... and finally began to gush over the hard, dry land of Iran.

Now there are eighty million people in Iran. And more and more of them every day are wanting to drink of the Living Water of Christ.

See Thinking Further for Cha ter 1 on page 135.

# 2. KURDS AND THE WAY
## (SAEED)

"Here it is," said Justin Perkins. "Right off the printing press." He held up a large sheet of paper, printed all over with a strange print. "The first Scriptures in our new written Syriac language."

The year was 1841. Justin Perkins, one of the first Western missionaries to Persia, had been translating the New Testament into modern Syriac for six years. Before long, the entire New Testament was printed.

Missionaries from among the Assyrian people of Persia began to leave Urmia to take the good news of Jesus Christ to other parts of the country. One of these was Pastor Yohannan. In 1879, he left for the town of Senneh, where the wild horseback-riding Kurds lived. The Kurds prided themselves on being very strict Muslims. They were willing to quickly kill any of their own if any of them turned away from the true faith and became infidels.

But, of course, no one ever did.

* * *

A sixteen-year-old Kurd named Saeed arrived at Pastor Yohannan's door in Senneh. He was going to teach Pastor Yohannan Persian, and Pastor Yohannan would teach him Syriac.

"I'll not greet those men with a *salaam* of peace," Saeed muttered to himself. "They're obviously infidels, unbelievers. Anyone who is not a Muslim will never receive the *salaam* of peace from me."

"Good morning," he said, when the door opened.

"You may give us the *salaam* of peace," said Pastor Yohannan's friend. "After all, we're People of the Book."[1]

*People of the Book?* Saeed glanced at the two of them sharply. *Then they know our holy Koran!* He knew that the Koran said that the Christian Bible was also a holy Book, and that the People of the Book—the Christians—were to be respected. But no Muslim did, really. It was unthinkable, because Christians didn't honor the Prophet Mohammed and the Koran. Saeed glanced down, unsure what to say.

The men were having their morning prayers. Before this time, Saeed had heard only Muslim prayers and superstitious Catholic prayers. How differently these men prayed! They bowed down on their knees and

---

1. "People of the Book" is an expression used in the Koran. Muslims who study the Koran know that the People of the Book are the Jews and Christians.

prayed as if they were praying to a real person, for forgiveness for sins, for their friends—and for their enemies! What good Muslim would do that?

Saeed looked at the Persian New Testament. "I've seen one of those," he said. "It didn't make any sense to me at all." He looked at Pastor Yohannan, who just smiled at him. *Some of those Christians have been my language students,* he thought. *Their lives don't match what they say they believe. You won't be any different.*

Months passed as the young teacher and the old student continued to meet together. More and more, Saeed found himself questioning, wondering, doubting.

He studied the prophecies of the Old Testament with Pastor Yohannan and saw that they pointed not to Mohammed, the bloody warrior, but to Jesus, the Prince of Peace.

And he watched the life of Pastor Yohannan, the Christian.

"How can this be?" Saeed muttered to himself, gripping his hair. "That Christian man is always kind and patient. He's always truthful, always! He knows his Scriptures very well and explains them with clear thinking. His whole life reflects all that he teaches! He never speaks badly of my people or my religion, though we speak badly of his people and his religion all the time! Why is this unbeliever so good, and we, the faithful ones, are not?"

In agony of soul, one day Saeed asked Pastor Yohannan plainly, "What do Christians think of our greatest prophet Mohammed, peace be upon him?"

For a moment, Pastor Yohannan was silent. He looked down.

"Really! I really do want to know!" Saeed insisted. "I won't harm you!"

Pastor Yohannan looked at Saeed with gentle eyes. "Jesus said that after Him would come false prophets. If you look honestly at Mohammed's life and character … We believe he's not a worthy example or a worthy prophet to represent the Holy God."

Pastor Yohannan's voice was so tender, so kind and loving, that in spite of the sting of his words, at first Saeed could not respond.

Finally he said, "Maybe you're mistaken."

Then passages from the Koran came to his mind, about Mohammed's violence and selfishness. *Not a worthy example. Not a worthy prophet. Maybe the pastor is right. Maybe you, Saeed, maybe you're wrong.*

Saeed left quickly and went home. "No!" he shouted to himself. "I dare not question my holy religion! I'll devote myself fully to it!" He sent the

Bible back to Pastor Yohannan and refused to come for studies.

Then he began to fast for the month of Ramadan. During the day, when everyone else was fasting and sleeping, he fasted and read the Koran. During the night, when everyone else was eating a big feast, he ate almost nothing. *Surely I'll find relief from these nagging thoughts!* But the doubts only became worse.

*What if the pastor is right? What if you're wrong? What if Mohammed was only an imposter?*

"No! No!" he screamed. "Satan has got my heart! I'm going to hell!"

In the middle of the night, Saeed jumped out of bed like a crazy man, ran to the fireplace, and pulled out two small red-hot charcoals. He put one on each leg and gritted his teeth and clenched his fists as he watched them burn. "That one is to remind me never to talk to another Christian!" he grunted through his clenched teeth. "And that one is to remind me that I will always and forever belong to holy Islam. Oh," he groaned. "How can an accursed Christian live a life holier than mine?"

In a few days, the pain in his legs passed. But the pain in his soul lingered on.

*Maybe the Christian is right. Maybe you're wrong.*

By day, Saeed taught his students the Koran. By night he prayed in the mosque. But the more he taught, the more he realized that the Koran was full of errors and bad teachings. The more he prayed, the more desperate he felt.

One night, walking home after prayers at the mosque, Saeed tripped over a stone and fell in the dirty street. Right there, in the dirt, he began to cry like a child. "O God," he called. "You said that You lead the lost. I'm lost. Show me the plain way. Show me the right way. I promise I'll follow it. If You don't—if I don't—I'll go completely crazy." He rested his head on his knees and sobbed.

In a moment, Saeed felt lifted up. In a moment, he knew exactly what he should do.

Early the next morning, he again knocked on the pastor's door. "Salaam, my friend," he said. "May I have the Bible again?"

"Saeed!" said Pastor Yohannan. "I'm so glad to see you! I've been praying for you. I know that God loves you."

Now Saeed studied the Bible, compared with the Koran, with an open heart, desperate to know the truth, to know the right way.

There came a day when he said, "Lord Jesus, I give you my whole heart and soul." Now his tears were no longer tears of grief and confusion and fear, but of an overwhelming sense of love and peace and joy. The Living Water had brought relief to his thirsty soul.

\* \* \*

When Saeed's relatives found out he had become a Christian, they wanted to kill him. He escaped to another city, where he studied medicine and became a doctor, giving many people the good news of Jesus Christ.

His brother finally found him in that city, determined to either force him to repent, or to kill him. But Saeed's brother was so impressed with his changed life and the good news of the gospel that he too became an ardent follower of Jesus Christ, taking the good news to many.

See Thinking Further for Chapter 2 on page 135.

# 3. WILD WOMAN IN THE DESERT (MARY BIRD)

"Khanum Maryam! Khanum Maryam! You must come quickly!"

Mary Bird looked up from her studying. Ever since she had arrived in Isfahan, Persia in 1891, she had been called away for one emergency after another. Persian women weren't allowed to see male doctors, and there weren't any female doctors. So whenever Mary could snatch a moment, she studied medicine to try to give what help she could.

Mary quickly grabbed her traveling cape and hurried out the door. "What is it?" she asked the young woman at the door. *A wife who had been beaten almost to death by her husband? A child with a cut that hadn't been cleaned properly that was now terribly infected? A woman dying in childbirth?*

"It's my mother, the woman with devils!" the young woman gasped. "She's wild! She'll kill everyone if we let her loose! You have to help her!"

Mary set her mouth firmly. Somehow they knew that the Christian doctor woman could do something. Well, by God's grace, she would.

"Where are we going?" Mary asked, as they rode out of town.

"They've chained her up outside of the town, in the desert," came the reply.

Mary remembered the Bible story of the demon-possessed man in the desert, who was healed by Christ. "Lord Jesus," she prayed. "Your healing power is the same yesterday, today, and forever. I'm Your willing worker. Show them Christ in me, the hope of glory."

There she was, the poor woman, chained to two large rocks, pulling against her chains and moaning. Mary's heart melted with love and concern.

"You poor thing," she murmured. "My God can heal you." She picked up her skirts and walked over to the rocks. "Dear, dear friend," she crooned. Gently she reached out to touch the woman's wild, matted hair.

The woman flinched, pulled back, and shrieked terribly.

"Dear, dear one," Mary whispered. "Has no one loved you in your sad life? Were you a child bride of a cruel husband? My God can heal you. My Jesus has love for you."

The woman moaned again and stopped pulling. Mary unchained her, and the woman began to flail, but she didn't run away.

"Holy Father, blessed Lord," Mary prayed, "this is a precious woman who needs Your healing touch. Heal her, touch her, our Great Physician."

Mary approached the woman again. "I love you, dear friend," she said, and kissed the woman on the cheek. She gently stroked her hair. "Have you ever felt a gentle touch?" she asked.

The woman's eyes opened wildly, and she moaned a moan that turned into a scream.

"Dear, dear," Mary murmured. "No need to scream. I'll sit with you until you feel better. May the Holy Spirit of Christ manifest Himself through me."

For over an hour, Mary sat with the wild woman, gently speaking of the love of God shown in Jesus Christ, praying, expressing her own love for her, and singing to her. The woman finally fell asleep on her shoulder.

Mary left her cloak behind as a pillow. "I've got to get back and get your mother some clothes," she told the daughter. "All she's wearing is rags. It's disgraceful."

"She'll just tear them up and throw them off," the daughter groaned.

"Even so," answered Mary. "But I don't think she will."

Mary returned with clothes, and helped the woman dress. The woman was quiet, and Mary sat with her, singing to her, speaking to her of the love of God.

It wasn't long before that same woman was able to go home. There she was, fully clothed and in her right mind, sitting next to her daughter.

"How can I ever thank you?" the woman murmured to Mary. "You came to me when my own people deserted me and left me in the desert to die."

"That's my Savior, Jesus Christ," Mary answered boldly. "He's the one to thank. He healed you. I was just His willing servant."

"Yes, your God is powerful," the woman answered. "Your religion must be true."

Throughout the city and the surrounding area, the news traveled. "Khanum Maryam healed the devil woman! Christianity must be very powerful!"

\* \* \*

Mary Bird worked as a pioneer missionary to women and a nurse for women in Persia for twenty years until her early death. The people grew to respect her and love her deeply. Though not many came to Christ under her ministry, many hearts were opened to see the true love and peace and righteousness of Christianity. Living Water was pouring out on a dry land.

See Thinking Further for Chapter 3 on page 136.

# 4. THE ONLY PROPHET THAT'S TRUE (RAJAB)

"I have to kill him. I have to just kill him." Rajab muttered the words to himself over and over.

Who would have thought that his revered teacher—the aged man who held so much wisdom—could utter such heresy? No wonder he had always avoided talking about religion! The conversations of the last few days swirled in Rajab's mind.

"Please tell me which religion you think is true," Rajab had begged him. "And which holy book you think is the right one."

The old man hesitated. "I've read many holy books," he said. "But the only prophet who impresses me as true is the prophet Jesus."

Rajab clutched his head in agony, remembering his teacher's words. How could it be? And how could the teacher have given so many convincing arguments after that? One after another after another. This man who knew their holy Koran so well had said, "In the Koran there are hundreds of stories empty of truth, never

25

recorded in history, opposite to logic, science, reason, and justice." And he had given example after example. This man who knew the holy Koran so well.

"I have to kill him," Rajab muttered again. Night and day he felt his soul torn in pieces. What should he do? He honored his teacher. What were the answers?

Finally he decided. *I'll study the Koran with the most dedicated mullahs. I'll find out the answers for myself. Then I'll kill him.*

For two years, Rajab studied the Koran at the feet of the men who honored it the most. The more he learned, the more he realized that the old teacher was right. Islam was full of confusion.

After two years, Rajab gave up. He didn't go back to the old teacher, but instead wandered in shadows of uncertainty. How could he possibly believe Islam any more? He looked at the Koran in his hand. How could he have thought it was holy?

He gazed into the night sky. If there was no Allah, was it all an accident? Was the creation of man just an accident too? Was there no purpose, no meaning? Was everything meaningless?

"Nothing is real," he decided. "There is no point or purpose to anything. After my heart finishes beating,

I'll die, and then I'll go nowhere. Life is without any meaning at all."

But with no purpose and no meaning, Rajab's life became as dark as a nightmare. "How can I escape from this?" he finally cried.

The words of the aged teacher came back to him, as if they were coming from far, far away. "The only prophet that impresses me as true is the prophet Jesus."

"I might as well hear what a Christian has to say," Rajab muttered. "At this point I have nothing to lose."

Rajab searched until he found where a Christian missionary lived, way out on the outskirts of town, almost in the desert. Three times he visited the house of that Christian missionary. Three times, for hours, he discussed these spiritual things with him. Finally he said to himself, "This will be the last night. I won't come here again."

But the third night, at the end, the missionary said, "Rajab, sin is like a terrible disease. All of mankind has this disease. There is only one medicine for it, and that's the gospel of Jesus Christ. You can accept it or reject it."

With a choke in his throat, Rajab arose to leave the missionary's house.

All around him, all he saw was empty wastelands. In his mind, he saw himself walking in a desert place.

Wandering, wandering, hopeless and lost, for the rest of his life. Maybe for eternity.

"O God!" he cried out suddenly, lifting his hands to the sky. "If You are real, and if Jesus is really from You, and if the gospel is really the medicine for the sickness of all mankind, then lead me to it! I don't know which direction to go! Which way is up? Which way is down?" His hands dropped heavily to his side. "If there is no God," he muttered, "then I have only spoken to the wind."

In an instant, Rajab saw a vision in the sky, two figures of sky-blue and shimmering. "God is real!" they said loudly. "Jesus is true! Be sure of that! And come!"

Then they disappeared.

Immediately Rajab felt waves of fear and nausea grip him. He began to sweat all over and tremble at the same time. Even in the heat, his teeth chattered.

He began to run. He ran and ran until finally he was in the center of town, with people all around. Then he stopped and looked around, breathing hard. People glanced at this strange fellow and went on their way.

Suddenly he realized he felt different. Completely different. *What happened to my confusion?* he thought. *What happened to my anger and depression and sorrow and despair and hopelessness? Now I'm filled with hope!*

The first thing Rajab did was to go and dig out the New Testament that the missionary had given him. He had tried to read it a little, but now he tried again.

It wasn't the same book any more. Now, it made sense!

"It's beautiful," he murmured. "And this Jesus, He says and does such extraordinary things!"

Rajab read the entire New Testament in four days. Almost every part seemed written just for him, to fulfill his own desires and to answer his questions. He began to know God.

Then he began reading the Old Testament, and more of his questions were answered. He began to see Jesus Christ for who He truly was, the only Savior of his soul. Rajab began to go to private places on purpose, just so he could dance and leap for joy.

"Glory and honor to Your Name, O God!" he cried. "You pour out grace, mercy, love, and compassion on the people of the earth. This medicine for the disease of sin doesn't just cure the illness to return me to the same old place. It brings me to a new place, a beautiful place! O my King, Lord Jesus Christ, You are glorious in power and might! You are my hope and my life and my confidence!"

Rajab searched and found the tiny Christian church in Tehran, the capital of the country. There he began

to worship with the other believers. There he grew in wisdom and knowledge, studying the Bible and praying with great power. Others around him heard what God had done for him and came to Christ.

When the time came for his baptism, in the summer of 1905, three missionaries gathered around him. "I want a new name when I'm baptized," he said. "I no longer want to be called Rajab, that Muslim name," he said. "But instead, call me Nozad, 'born again.' That will be my name from now on. On that deserted street, when the vision appeared to me, God began a work in me and brought me to Himself. I'll never forget how He brought me from darkness to light, from a world of death to a world of life. Jesus is the prophet who is true, and I am born again. I am Nozad."

\* \* \*

Nozad became an eager evangelist. He traveled far and wide throughout Iran to tell others about the great love of the Savior, Jesus Christ.

See Thinking Further for Chapter 4 on page 136.

# 5. SOWING SEED IN A DESERT PLACE (WILLIAM MILLER)

"Why am I here, Lord?" William Miller looked all around him at the barren region of Seistan.

The young missionary had come from America in 1919, only two years earlier, to start a mission in the city of Mashhad, a city considered holy by all Muslims. But now, because enemy forces were threatening to invade, William and the other missionaries had been forced to walk or ride through the cold winter weather over five hundred miles to safety. For days and weeks they had plodded on.

And now, this was their safe place; a barren desert area, with a few sad-looking buildings left over from the Great War.

"The doctors and nurses can help sick people get well. But what can I do here?" William asked God.

William found someone to help him continue his studies of the Persian language. But none of the beggars or nomads, who came to the clinic, showed any interest in the stories he read about Jesus in the waiting room.

They just wanted to see the doctors and nurses for their sick children.

All the men wore huge, heavy black beards, so William decided to let his red beard grow long and bushy. But still, when he walked through the marketplace to try to sell or give away the Scriptures in their language, most of the people shook their heads, uninterested. Most of them couldn't read anyway. Only a few, out of curiosity, offered him the few cents that he asked in exchange for the Holy Word of God.

One day, in the bazaar, an old man called from outside his shop, "Come! Tell me about those books!"

William came, eager to read the stories about the miracles of Jesus.

Other men began to gather. "Those are good, those are good," they said, nodding their heads.

Then William turned to John chapter 3, the story of Nicodemus coming to Jesus at night. " As Moses lifted up the serpent in the wilderness,'" he read, "'even so must the Son of Man be lifted up.' That means that Jesus had to die on the cross."

"Die on the cross?" said one man. "No. That's ridiculous."

"But this is the way God made for our sins to be cleansed and for us to have …" William couldn't finish his sentence.

"No," interrupted the men, waving their hands. "That's the ridiculous notion of the Christians. Your book is corrupted. Everybody knows Jesus didn't really die on the cross. Why would a prophet die on a cross? That's ridiculous." They stood up and walked away, talking loudly among themselves.

Sadly William looked down at the text. *Eternal life.* Those were the next words he was going to say. *For us to have eternal life.*

*For God so loved the world* ... The words swam before his misty eyes. The men were gone. *God, will there be any harvest here? Will no one listen?*

The wind of the desert blew and blew and blew for months, blowing dust into the mouth and eyes and nose of anyone too foolish not to hold a handkerchief over his face. For almost a year, William remained in this desert place. Even after the other missionaries went back, he stayed several months longer. *God, surely You don't intend for Your Living Water to just evaporate in the sun, do You? Don't You want to see a harvest here?*

But the people went on about their lives—to him, it seemed almost as if they thought he was invisible. Had anyone listened to anything he had said? It didn't seem so. Sadly he returned to Mashhad to rejoin the other missionaries.

\* \* \*

Years later, a Persian Christian friend named Hopeful went from Mashhad to Seistan, that desert place, to sell Bibles. When he returned, he said, "There's a Christian in Seistan! And he's a chief of some of the tribal people! He invites other chiefs to come to his house to read the Bible!"

"That's wonderful news!" William responded. "How did he come to Christ? Where did he get that Bible?"

"I don't know, but everyone knows he's a Christian. He isn't afraid to proclaim it."

More years went by while William Miller worked in the city of Mashhad. Finally, in 1941, more than twenty years after his first trip to Seistan, William

and Hopeful were able to travel the five hundred miles down to Seistan again. "I certainly would like to meet that Christian chief," William murmured.

The two men sold a few Bibles and other Christian books, and visited the missionaries that now lived in the area.

On the last day of their visit, in the marketplace, Hopeful ran up to William. "I found him!" he exclaimed. "The Christian chief! He wants to meet with you!"

With excitement, William prepared for the meeting. But instead of a burly, loud, fearsome chief, William met a man whose hair was combed and who greeted him with a peaceful "Salaam."

"How long have you been a Christian, sir?" William asked. "Who told you about Jesus?"

Chief Nazar Khan said, "I've been a Christian for a long time. Twenty years. But no one told me."

William's face showed his confusion. "Then how did you learn about Him?"

"Through the Bible," the chief answered, smiling. "The Bible that you gave me. But I think then you had a big red beard, is that right?"

"Yes, yes!" William said. He searched his memories of his barren visit to Seistan over twenty years earlier, trying to place this face, this voice. When had he given a Bible to this man?

The chief chuckled. "I was very young, coming to the market from a distant village. You had a Persian Bible. I wanted one. You told me, 'This is the Word of God. Take good care of it.'"

William's memory went back to the few people in Seistan who had shown any interest at all in the Word of God, who had taken the book out of curiosity and given him the few cents he asked. He never knew, of course, what they did with it when they got home.

"I took that Bible home," the chief said, "and read the whole thing. I believed in Jesus Christ. Seven years later, a missionary came through the area and baptized me. I hung a cross on my door so everyone would know I had become a Christian. When the other chiefs wanted to go to war, I talked them out of it, because Jesus taught us peace. I have not been silent about my faith." He leaned back and smiled.

*You did this, Lord!* William's heart sang. *That seemed like the driest time of all my years as a missionary, when no one at all was listening. But even so, You had soil prepared to receive Your seed. You had hearts prepared to receive Your Living Water!*

\* \* \*

William Miller continued in missionary work in Persia, later called Iran, from 1919 until 1962. He appears again in chapters 6 and 8.

See Thinking Further for Chapter 5 on page 137.

# 6. STONE THE VICTORIOUS ONE (HASAN)

"They're hoping for a miracle. Well, we'll give them one, all right!"

Twelve-year-old Hasan and his friends looked out over the milling crowds of people gathered at the shrine of Imam Reza. That shrine was what made this city, Mashhad, a holy city. They came with their prayers, looking for answers, looking for miracles. There were stories that at this tomb, the blind would receive their sight, the deaf would hear, and the lame would walk.

But none of those were the kind of miracle that would happen today.

"Hey, you camels," Hasan and his friends crooned, sneaking up on the weary animals. The camels had come a long way, and were now kneeling in a group outside the milling throng of people, quietly eating. The keeper sat under a tree, asleep.

Each boy reached into his sack and pulled out a handful of burrs. Quietly and carefully he placed each one under the tail of an unsuspecting camel.

"Hey! Hey!" the boys called, stepping back and slapping the camels right on the burrs. Suddenly the camels all leaped up, frantically racing in circles, trying to get the burrs out from under their tails. All of them raced out the gate and down the street, straight to the shrine.

"A miracle!" the gatekeeper called. "Camels have made the pilgrimage to the shrine!" And all the trumpets blared to show that even animals respected and honored the Imam Reza.

"Huh," grunted Hasan. "Bunch of fools."

Over the years, the foolishness and lies and wickedness he saw in Muslims turned Hasan more and more away from the religion of his homeland. When he was a young man, he decided to investigate a new religion, Baha'i, to find out if it was true. He traveled two thousand miles, walking much of the way. Finally he reached the home of Abdul-Baha, the head of this religion. There he stayed for over two months.

"Yes, this is the true religion," Abdul-Baha assured him. "My father was a manifestation of God. This

religion will replace Islam." He taught Hasan, but he also let him stay at his house and gave him sweets to eat and let him ride in his fancy carriage.

One day a poor person came to the door of Abdul-Baha's house, asking for money.

"No, turn him away," Abdul-Baha told his servant.

One day one of the servants failed to finish a job well enough. Abdul-Baha hit him and cursed him.

Hasan left Abdul-Baha and traveled back to his home in Mashhad. *The Muslim religion can't be true*, he said to himself. *And the way that 'Manifestation of God' treated other people showed me that this Baha'i religion can't be true either. I guess there is no God and no truth.*

Hasan tried to forget about the darkness in his soul and lived just for money and all that it could give him. He became a traveling merchant.

On one of his journeys, Hasan came to a stall where a man sat surrounded by books, reading to a few other men who had gathered around him. Hasan was curious.

"Are you selling books?" he asked. He had never seen so many books at once.

"Yes," answered the man. "But they cost only a few cents. Can you read?"

"I've never needed to," Hasan answered gruffly. "I'm a merchant."

"Then come and join us," said the man kindly. He was Benjamin Badal, an Assyrian missionary from the northern part of Iran who had been trained by Justin Perkins.

Benjamin continued his reading from the Gospel of Matthew. He was reading chapter 24.

"And Jesus answered and said to them, 'Be careful to let no man deceive you. For many shall come in My name, saying, "I am the Anointed One from God," and shall deceive many.' "

Hasan nodded, listening, thinking, while Benjamin read.

Then he heard him read, " 'And many false prophets shall rise, and they shall deceive many.' "

Hasan sat upright. *I know that!* he thought. *I know about those false prophets—Mohammed is one! I know about those false Anointed Ones—Abdul-Baha is one!*

When Benjamin finished his reading, Hasan asked, "Who said these words?"

"The prophet Jesus," Benjamin answered. "He said them."

*Then, Jesus must be the true prophet!* Hasan thought. "Here, can I buy one of those?"

"Yes, this is the Gospel of Matthew. Will you be able to find someone to read it to you?"

"Oh yes, yes, certainly." He took the book and went on his way.

* * *

Hasan traveled around the country for years, buying and selling. In all the different cities, whenever he met any Christians, he asked them to read to him from the Gospel of Matthew. He listened and knew these were the true words. He heard them so many times that he memorized the whole book. He believed in Jesus Christ with his whole heart.

* * *

Finally, in 1920, when he was about fifty years old, Hasan finally returned to his home in Mashhad. There he found that missionaries had set up work in his home city. One of them was William Miller.

"I'm a Christian," he declared boldly to the missionaries. "I've trusted in the Jesus of this book. I want to be baptized. And I want a new name. I no longer want to be called Hasan, a Muslim name, but rather Mansur the Victorious One." He took as his last name Sang, which means "stone," like Simon Peter's name. He became Stone the Victorious One.

Stone the Victorious One, never learned to read, but he memorized so much of the New Testament that it didn't matter. After his baptism, he said, "I've traveled all my life. Now I'll travel in the service of my Savior." He began walking throughout the country of

Iran, thousands and thousands of miles, giving away Gospels so that other people could hear the good news.

"I'm like the sower in Matthew 13!" he chuckled. "This is my seed! 'The seed is the Word of God.' I'm sowing it wherever I go." And off he went from one village to the next, his back laden down with a pack of booklets to give away.

"How can you believe that false prophet, Mohammed?" he thundered out in one village after another. "Believe the true Word of God in Jesus Christ!" The village people shouted curses at him, the dogs chased him, but here and there a few people secretly took the books he offered, and here and there a few gatherings of new believers began to read the books together.

Through the scorching sun and dry desert winds and freezing cold of winter, Stone the Victorious One kept going, year after year. His long black beard grew thin and wispy gray.

"Mansur is in town!" the Christians would call to each other with joy.

"Mansur! Mansur!" the children of the Christians called.

"Little ones!" Mansur called back. He took off his cap and waved it happily. "Ha ha! I am here!"

"Come inside, my brother, and clean off the fleas and lice," one of the Christian brothers would call. "We have some fresh clothes for you."

And so it went for the next sixteen years. When Mansur died in 1936, hundreds of Christians came to his funeral. Dr. Saeed, the Kurd who had found Jesus Christ (mentioned in Chapter 2), conducted his funeral. Few Iranian Christians were so fully committed to Jesus Christ as was Stone the Victorious One.

See Thinking Further for Chapter 6 on page 137.

# 7. CHRISTIAN DOGS (HOSSEIN, PART ONE)

"Hey, Hossein!" The boy's uncle called from the doorway.

Four-year-old Hossein came running. "Yes, Uncle?"

"I saw you talking to those Christian dogs!" His uncle leaned down till his face was only inches from the boy's. "Don't ever talk to them, you hear me? There is nothing lower on this earth." He leaned down and shook his finger in the boy's face. "Don't you ever—" his face grew bright red "—*ever* talk to those vile, filthy Christian dogs again! Don't even go near them!" He spat on the ground.

Hossein nodded at his uncle without a word. He turned to look at his four-year-old friends. They were Christian dogs.

By the time Hossein was seven, he had learned his lesson well. He hated the Christians in his city of Mashhad, and he spat at them when they walked by.

There was one of the vile, filthy Christian women who used to be a Muslim, returning from the well.

What kind of low, revolting scum was she? She set her waterpot down in front of her house. Hossein's heart filled with hatred for her. He picked up a large stone and hurled it at the waterpot.

Crash! A piece flew out of the pot, and a crack appeared all the way from the top to the bottom. Water began to pour out onto the ground. Hossein turned to run away.

Oof! Where had that *other* large stone come from? The boy tumbled to the ground, scraping the skin off his knee. Blood began to pour out. He gritted his teeth to keep from crying.

"Boy!" the woman called.

*Oh no, she'll get me!* Hossein felt sudden panic. *I've got to get up and run away!* He tried to stumble to his feet again.

There she was, towering over him! He closed his eyes and held his hands before his face to protect himself from her blows.

"No, no, I won't hurt you," the woman said. "Here, let me help you." To his astonishment, the woman helped him up. "You've got a bad scrape there." She didn't even mention the waterpot. *Hadn't she noticed it? Surely she'd seen it!*

"Come here, I can clean your wound for you," she said. With great gentleness she applied a cool cloth to wipe out the sand and pebbles in his knee. Hossein kept his face down, glancing up at her only occasionally. Her face was kind.

"There, there, it will be all right," she said as she applied some medicine and a bandage. "Here, get up. I have something for you. You can eat it."

She held out a piece of candy.

How could this be? How could a Christian dog act in such a kind way? Hossein didn't understand this woman's kindness.

But he never forgot it.

* * *

Twelve years later, in 1955, Hossein, now a young man, was fighting his required two years in the Iranian army. He became very sick with an infection and a high fever and had to go to the hospital.

"Hello, Hossein."

Hossein turned his head from gazing out the window to the door of his hospital room. "Hello," he murmured.

Why was it that the only one of his army buddies who would visit him in the hospital was this Christian?

"I wanted you to know that I've been praying for your healing." The young friend smiled.

Hossein nodded slightly. He didn't know what to say. What do you say to a Christian dog who prays for you?

The two friends talked for a few minutes. But when the friend left, he pressed something into Hossein's hand. "This is to help you remember who the Healer is," he said.

Hossein opened his hand. It was a small wooden cross. He should have thrown it across the room and cursed at Jesus and all those Christian dogs. But instead he just gazed at it.

"Thank you," he murmured.

The friend left, and Hossein fell into a fitful sleep. For hours he tossed and turned with his high fever.

"Hossein," said a voice. It was a voice calling him from somewhere. He couldn't tell where.

"Who are you? What do you want?" called Hossein.

"I am Jesus Christ," said the voice. "Arise and eat."

In his dream, Hossein took the food that lay before him. For the first time in weeks, he could eat and enjoy it. He felt strengthened by the food.

The next morning, Hossein's bed was covered with sweat. The fever had finally broken. He lay there looking at the ceiling. "I'm well," he murmured. "The infection is gone." He could just feel it in his body—it was healed.

Then he had to admit what had happened. He had to say it out loud to himself.

"Jesus Christ healed me."

He got up from the bed and prepared to leave the hospital.

*Jesus Christ healed me,* he kept murmuring to himself. How did he know that for certain? He wasn't even sure how he knew it, but he knew it. He knew it. The prophet Jesus, He had appeared to him, to Hossein. He had told him to arise and eat. Then he was well! That was all he knew.

All the other soldiers had been ordered to fight somewhere else by now. Hossein was alone in this city. But he had to find out more about Jesus.

Who could he ask?

"Is there a Christian church in this city?" he asked people on the streets. But none of them knew anything about it. Why was a Muslim looking for a Christian church anyway?

Then Hossein saw a man wearing the robe of an Armenian. Surely he would know. "Please," he asked, "can you tell me where I'll find a Christian church?"

"Yes," said the man. "Meet me on Sunday morning, and I'll take you there."

Week after week, Hossein went to that church. He asked many questions of the pastor, who always answered them patiently. "See," said the pastor, "when Jesus told you in your dream to arise and eat, He was saying something similar to what He said in John 6. You must eat His flesh and drink His blood. This means that, in all ways, He will be a part of your very being."

"Arise and eat," murmured Hossein. He listened and studied the Bible. He studied the book of John, especially chapter 6. This Jesus was surely more than just a prophet.

Finally there came a day when Hossein said, "I will put all my faith and trust in Jesus Christ, the Living God. I will renounce the ways of Islam!" His heart was flooded with love and light.

It was a long time before Hossein was able to travel the thousand miles back to his home of Mashhad to tell his parents about his conversion to Christianity, his salvation. What would they say? Would his uncle call him a Christian dog? Hossein's heart pounded in his chest. *My Father in heaven, I pray that they'll know what a loving God You are. But if they refuse You, I only ask that I stand strong. I love my family, but I love my Savior even more.*

See Thinking Further for Chapter 7 on page 138.

# 8. ARISE AND EAT!
# (HOSSEIN, PART TWO)

When Hossein arrived at his home, he first greeted all of his family with hugs and smiles. Then he began the speech he had prepared.

"Uncle, I have some very good news." He could feel his heart pounding, but still, somehow, he felt peace. "I've found the answers to many of our life questions."

Hossein's uncle looked quizzical, guarded. "What do you mean, my son?"

"I've found the true salvation of my soul. Back when I was so sick in the hospital, a prophet appeared to me in a dream and told me to arise and eat. Then I was healed."

"Which prophet was it?" Hossein's uncle still seemed guarded, his arms folded across his chest.

"It was the prophet *Isa*. Jesus Christ."

Hossein's uncle stood silent, his eyebrows lifted.

"Jesus Christ has shown me the way to the true God. He has shown me that He is God Himself. I'm a Christian, and now I've found—"

But Hossein couldn't say anymore. His uncle slapped him across his mouth.

"You are *not!*" his uncle yelled. "You are a Muslim, and you will *never* be a Christian! How *dare* you utter such blasphemy! You will renounce this Christianity today, right now, this minute!"

Hossein stood stunned, as more and more of his family members began to gather from other parts of the house. They all stood speechless as well, their eyes wide.

For days the family begged and pleaded and wept. His uncle yelled. Hossein spoke little, and prayed. "I cannot. I can't turn my back on my Savior. If you only knew—" But his uncle wouldn't let him continue.

Finally the day came that his uncle said, "You will leave our house, and you are never welcome back here. You are no longer part of our family."

As Hossein sat on the bus on the way to Tehran, he stared out the window. His uncle's words kept ringing in his ears. "You are no longer part of our family."

*I no longer have a family. I can no longer enjoy laughter and love with them.* It seemed impossible to grasp, impossible to understand. What would he do?

He loved his mother and his uncle. He loved his brothers and sisters.

But he loved Jesus more.

In Tehran, Hossein found his Christian friend and his family, who welcomed him as if he were their brother. In fact, they knew that he was.

Hossein became a street peddler for a living, but he didn't care about trying to get rich. He wanted the riches of Christ. He eagerly listened to all that the Christians around him taught. He studied the Bible and prayed every night at the nightly prayer meetings. Together they prayed and prayed and prayed.

"Hossein, you're so dedicated to Christ," one of the church leaders said one day, "we'd like for you to attend Bible school. It's up in the mountains outside Tehran, and it's taught by a Godly old man, a missionary from America who's been here for decades. His name is William Miller."

"That sounds like a dream come true," said Hossein. "But how would I pay for it? How would I pay for a place to live, and for food?"

"Christians in the United States are sending money to support this missionary and his Bible school. By the way, Hossein, I know you're from Mashhad. This man, William Miller, has been a missionary in Mashhad for forty years. When you broke that Christian woman's water pot, it may well have been a woman he taught. He's a good man. He truly loves God, and he knows His Holy Word."

For two years, all Hossein did was learn the Bible from William Miller and other teachers, with other young men who were also eager to learn. He loved it. For two years he was able to "arise and eat" early every morning of the Living Word of God, Jesus Christ. For two years he drank in the Living Water, Jesus Christ. Then for years he traveled all over Iran, taking the good news of Jesus Christ, giving away books or selling them for just a little bit of money. He married and had children and continued to travel and serve God.

But in 1979, all of Iran changed. Many violent young people helped to overthrow the government of Iran and bring in the new leader, the Ayatollah Khomeini. They believed the lies that by using war, violence, and bloodshed to bring in real Islam, they would bring perfect peace and justice to Iran.

But perfect peace and justice didn't happen. Instead, the country became so filled with violence and corruption that it was like a nightmare. When some of the former revolutionaries finally tried to stand up to the corrupt leaders, the soldiers of the new Islamic government seized them and tortured them.

The new Islamic government declared that they would wipe out all Christian missions to Muslims. They especially hated anyone who used to be a Muslim who now called himself a Christian.

But Hossein wasn't afraid. "I believe the Holy Spirit is speaking to me," he said to his wife one day. "I believe He wants us to move back to Mashhad, the city of my birth, and start a church there."

"How will we start a church there?" his wife asked. "It's against the law to start a church without being registered with the government."

"The Lord will lead us every step of the way," Hossein answered. "All the people who come to us, we'll disciple them the way my Christian mentors discipled me. I believe the Holy Spirit is telling us that's what we need to do. People are angry about what the Iranian Revolution has done to our great country, especially the young people, I think. They were promised a great new world, but all they're getting is fear. They see this terrible oppression, and they think, this is the best possible world? They're hungry for something real, something that will fill the emptiness of their souls. They want to arise and eat."

Christians in Mashhad, especially students at the University of Mashhad, whispered an invitation to someone else, or handed someone a little slip of paper with a note on it. Sneaking from different roads and at different times, people entered the tiny basement apartment to sit cram-packed next to each other. They came to listen to the man of God speak the words of God, to try to understand the hope of this wonderful news.

Many of them found what they were looking for. So they came to renounce Islam, to lift their hands in worship of the true God, with tears streaming down their faces.

Through the powerful life and teaching of Hossein Soodmand, Jesus Christ was shown to be the true Savior. For one hungry, thirsty Muslim after another, Jesus Christ was the Living Bread and the Living Water.

*Come fill your cup. Arise and eat.*

\* \* \*

Throughout the 1980s, only about fifteen or twenty regular church members, almost all of them believers from a Muslim background, met in Hossein's house church. Along with them came a constant stream of visitors, sometimes dozens at a time. Hossein Soodmand's story intertwines with the stories of chapters 9-13.

See Thinking Further for Chapter 8 on page 138.

# 9. THE MYSTERIOUS BOOK (MINA, PART ONE)

*What's that?* seventeen-year-old Mina thought to herself as she picked up the book off the library floor. *Hmmm. It's not a library book.*

*Injil Sharif,* the book said. Holy Good News?

"I've heard of this," she said to herself. "I think it's the holy book of the Christians. And it's in our language. I had no idea there were any copies of that book in Persian. I thought it was only in French and English."

It was the mid-1980s. The Iranian Revolution had happened just a few years earlier. The country of Iran had changed so completely, with great violence and fear and oppressive laws, that almost all Bibles had been destroyed. Mina had never even seen a New Testament, or even heard that it had been translated into Persian over 150 years earlier.

Immediately Mina took the book to the librarian. "Did someone lose this book?" she asked.

The librarian took the book and turned it front and back, examining it. "No one has reported losing a book like this one," she answered. "Take it with you. You can read it and study it at home."

*Read it and study it at home?* Mina thought. *What an odd thing to say!* She stuffed the book in her backpack, curious to learn more.

That evening, Mina arrived home to find her family sitting around the front room reading, as usual. "Look!" She held up the book for her parents and sister and brother-in-law to see. "I found this in the library, and the librarian said I could keep it! It's a holy book!"

To Mina's surprise, her father jumped from his chair and grabbed her arm. At the same time, her brother-in-law grabbed the book. "It's the Christian Bible in Persian!" he cried.

Mina could see the anger in her father's face. "Where did you get that?" he asked.

The girl's own face flushed red with embarrassment and self-defense. "I told you! I found it in the library, and the librarian said I could keep it. It's not a bad book, is it?"

Her father's face still showed great anger. "We respect that book, but it is not our holy book. Our holy book is the Koran. You don't need another holy book. Take it back to the library—don't make me take it back myself! Never touch books like that again. Do you understand?"

Mina trembled with embarrassment and fear and confusion. She felt humiliated for being rebuked in front of all the family. Her father was usually so kind— she had never seen him act this way.

The silence lay heavy and thick in the room. Mina's mother shifted in her chair uncomfortably. *No, I don't understand!* Mina's heart shouted loudly. But in her fear she murmured, "Yes."

Finally the younger brother broke the silence. "Father, why are you so angry?" he asked. "Why is it wrong just to find out what other people believe?"

"No daughter of mine will ever read a Bible!" Father sputtered. "Everything you need, you can find in the Koran." He glared at Mina.

Mina's brother-in-law added, "You must be strong, Mina, to resist the temptation to look at anything that might lead you away from your noble Islamic faith."

*What's wrong with everyone?* Mina thought desperately. *What could possibly be so bad about this book?* "I'll do as you say," she whispered. In tears, she ran off to her room and closed the door.

Later that night, Mina's mother came to the door and peeked in. "Daughter," she whispered, "don't forget your promise to take the book back."

Mina's face was red with weeping, and she was still shaking. But she looked up and said, "Mother, wouldn't *you* like to read that book?"

Mother gently repeated the words Father had said earlier. "Everything we need, we can find in the Koran." She closed the door.

*What can be so terrible about a holy book that my parents respect?* Mina struggled within herself. Would she obey and return the book to the library as she had been told to do? Or would she disobey?

Slowly, with her lips set in a thin line, she pulled out a flashlight from her drawer, opened the *Injil*, and began to read.

Early the next morning when Mother called her for breakfast, Mina awoke with a panic. The flashlight was still on! She had fallen asleep reading the *Injil!* Where was it? Her heart raced as she saw that it had fallen off her bed and lay in the middle of the floor in her room. What if someone had come in? What would have happened to her?

Quickly she stuffed the New Testament under her mattress and hurried to breakfast.

Over the next two nights, under the covers with the flashlight, Mina read the entire New Testament.

Who was this man called Jesus? He didn't fight wars to extend His power the way Mohammed did—His power was extended without the sword! He didn't collect many wives the way Mohammed did—He didn't have even one! He never robbed people the way Mohammed did, he treated women with respect, He did miracles, He spoke with wisdom and kindness. Kindness. Kindness. So different from Mohammed.

"And I can read it in my own language," Mina murmured. "It always made me mad that I had to learn a different language to read the Koran and to say my prayers." She remembered the questions of her youth that had frustrated her father. "Why can't Allah understand our own language? Why does Allah have to have everything in Arabic? Is Allah a racist?"

But there were still so many questions. What did Jesus mean when He said He would give rest to those who are burdened? Was He talking about the burdens of religion?

*If there's an Injil in Persian, then that means there must be some Christians in my country,* Mina thought. *I need to meet them. I need to understand this better. I'm still a Muslim, of course, because that's my life, but I want to understand the Injil better. I want to know more about this prophet Jesus.*

Mina continued her prayers to Allah just as she always did. She spread her prayer rug and bowed down again and again, kneeling toward Mecca. But for years now, she had felt as if Allah was not hearing her prayers.

"God, do you hear me?" she cried one day. "I'm stuck with no freedom to choose my own way. I've tried so hard through the years to please You, but I'm exhausted. Please, if you care about me, show me."

That night, Mina had a dream.

She wandered alone in a twilight-misty desert, dying of thirst. Suddenly a voice, seeming to be from nowhere, cried out, "I am the way, and the truth, and the life! No one comes to the Father except through me!"[1]

Mina sat up with a shock, suddenly awake. Who was that voice? "I have to find a follower of Jesus to explain things to me!" she cried out. "But how?"

Not long after, some relatives came to visit. One of them was Monir, ten years older than Mina, and like a big sister to her. Mina loved talking with Monir, but this time when they went into Mina's room together, Mina gasped. She had forgotten and left the Bible out on the table! She glanced over with fear in her eyes. What would Monir say? Monir's family were even stricter Muslims than her own!

But to Mina's surprise, her cousin almost ran to the Bible and hugged it to herself. "Mina!" she whispered. "Do you read this book?"

---

1. John 14:6

Mina felt as if she were in a dream. Monir knew about the *Injil?* She told her cousin the whole story, including the voice she heard in the night and her desire to find a follower of Jesus.

"I am a follower of Jesus!" Monir exclaimed. "I have been for several years, ever since I studied at the University of Mashhad. That was where I was invited to a special meeting of Christians. I knew what those young people had was real. I asked Jesus right there, at that first meeting, to change my life too, and He has!" Her face glowed with joy. "I still wear all these things—" she pointed to all the cloths that covered her head and hair and face and body "—but in my heart I'm not a Muslim. I'm a Christian. Listen, Mina, keep asking Jesus to show Himself to you, and He will, because He is alive! Hallelujah!"

Mina's head was spinning as the two young women left their bedroom to rejoin the family. She could hardly begin to grasp the huge secret they now shared.

See Thinking Further for Chapter 9 on page 139.

# 10. WHO IS THAT YOUNG MAN?
## (MINA, PART TWO)

Before long, Monir invited Mina to go out for an afternoon with her. Mina's parents thought they were just going out shopping—they didn't know that the two young women were planning to attend a secret meeting of Christians in someone's small apartment.

There, for the first time in her life, Mina heard people sing worship songs. *Strange and beautiful,* she thought. *Look how happy and peaceful they are!*

Then in the short Bible talk that someone gave, Mina heard for the first time that all people are sinners. *How kind they are to me, even though I'm Muslim!* she thought. *I know that if they went to a mosque, the leaders there wouldn't treat them this way!*

Mina met with Monir every chance she got, and made every excuse she could to attend the secret meetings. But at the same time, she continued to do her prayer rituals. She studied hard and got high grades in school. Her parents had no clue about her secret life.

"Listen, Mina!" Monir said over the phone one day. "A Christian pastor from Mashhad is coming to Tehran on Thursday to be our speaker at our secret meeting. I'm so excited, because he's the pastor who first gave me the gospel! Pastor Hossein Soodmand! Can you come?"

Mina's heart pounded. She had never seen a real Christian pastor, not in person. "Yes, I'll be there!" she whispered.

In that tiny apartment, so many people gathered that they were all sitting shoulder to shoulder. They gazed at Pastor Soodmand's face, so different from the angry leaders of Islam, radiating peace and joy. He spoke on and on about the love of Jesus Christ for all.

Mina felt it. She felt the warmth of that love all through her body. She felt the room begin to glow with a glorious light.

How many years she had prayed for Allah to show himself to her like this—he never had. But now ...!

In the middle of the sermon, Mina slid to the floor and cried out, "I want to give my heart to Jesus! Hallelujah! Hallelujah! I want to belong to Jesus Christ!" She began to sob.

Pastor Soodmand rushed to her side. "Are you ready to turn from Islam and all the Islamic heroes?"

"Yes, yes!" Mina sobbed.

"Repeat this in a loud voice," said Pastor Soodmand. And Mina repeated in a loud voice. "Lord Jesus, today I confess my sins! I want to repent of all of them in Your Name! You are the Savior of the world! This day I give my heart to you! I believe that You died on the cross for me and that God raised You from death on the third day! I turn from all false prophets and all other religions, because I choose You this day as my Savior and Lord. In Jesus' Name, amen!"

Mina's body continued to tremble as she sobbed with joy and love, feeling overwhelmed with the light and love of Christ.

Now, at the Thursday night meetings, Mina was no longer simply an observer, a questioner. Now she was a full worshiper. Her heart overflowed with love for this Savior who had loved her so much. He had died for her, even when she was a sinner. She loved gathering with the secret believers, and she often was able to talk with Pastor Soodmand on the phone for encouragement and wisdom. She read the Bible over and over, and with the help of Monir and other Christians, gained answers to her questions and began to help other seekers with their questions.

And still her parents didn't know.

The time had come when Mina was growing old enough to marry. Many rich and powerful Muslim men, young and old, handsome and plain, came to ask her father's permission to marry her. But her father refused them all. Until one night . . .

"Mina," Father said. He was knocking on Mina's door, so she quickly hid her Bible under her mattress. "Yes, Father?"

He entered the room. "A young man named Javid has asked to pursue you in marriage. He remembers seeing you at the library. I like him—he seems truthful. Is this acceptable with you?"

Mina's memory went back to a time when a handsome young man had watched her. Was he the one? Her heart pounded. But suddenly she felt filled with peace.

"Yes, Father," she said. If she married a younger man, he might be more open to discussing new spiritual ideas than an old man would be.

The two families met, and within hours Mina and Javid were engaged. They sat across the room smiling at each other as their families discussed the terms of the engagement. Mina's heart pounded again. What would her new husband think when he found out that she was a worshiper of Jesus Christ?

Later, she made a secret phone call. "Monir?" She spoke quietly. "I know we usually go to the Thursday meetings, but I want to go to the Monday meeting this week since Pastor Soodmand will be there. I want to talk to him about my engagement. I think he'll understand about how I have to marry a Muslim, and he'll encourage me."

The next week, Mina entered the small apartment for the Monday night meeting, full of Christians that she hadn't met before. Suddenly she stopped, in shock.

There sat Javid, the man she was going to marry.

Javid jumped up. "What are you doing here?" he asked in astonishment.

Mina recovered herself. "What are *you* doing here?" Was he here to spy on her?

"Mina, I'm a Christian! I believe in Jesus Christ!" Javid said. Then he said it again, louder. "I've trusted in Jesus Christ for my salvation. I'm a believer!"

Mina gasped. "I am too! Jesus Christ is my Savior and Lord!"

Pastor Soodmand quickly came over to them. "Do you two know each other?" he asked.

"Yes!" they both cried out. "We're getting married in four days!"

Pastor Soodmand stopped and looked at both of them. Then he lifted his face and hands to heaven. "Lord, look what you've done!" he rejoiced. "I knew that both of these young people were getting married, and I was praying for both of them, and their future mates. But this … I didn't know! Look what You've done!" And tears began to flow down his face.

For hours and hours the Christians in that little apartment sang and sang and worshiped and worshiped. Oh, look what God had done!

\* \* \*

Years later, Mina and Javid (whose story is in the next chapter) had to escape from Iran for their lives. While they were in Holland, a kind Iranian translator listened to Mina's story of how she found the *Injil* and came to Christ.

The lady then said to her, "I thought you looked familiar, and now I know why. I was the one who left that *Injil* under the table, and I was the one who told you to take it home to read. I was that librarian."

See Thinking Further for Chapter 10 on page 139.

# 11. THE RELUCTANT SOLDIER (JAVID, PART ONE)

"No, I don't want to fight in this horrible war!" Javid muttered as he held the paper before him. "I just want to study at the university! I don't want to kill anybody!"

But the paper he had received told him that if he didn't go fight in the war against Iraq, he would no longer be able to buy a house or a car, study at a university, or have a job. It was an impossible situation.

The year was 1980, at the beginning of the war between Iran and Iraq, shortly after the Ayatollah had taken over the land of Iran. Every young man had to fight in the army for at least two years, whether he wanted to or not. Many didn't want to. But they had no choice.

With very little training, Javid and his whole unit were stationed at the very worst fighting. In the heat of the fighting, only three of Javid's group survived. He was one of the survivors.

"I've got to get out of here," Javid murmured. "I've got to get out. I've got to go someplace and get some help. I'm desperate."

*Mashhad. I'll go to the holy city of Mashhad and pray at the tomb of Imam Reza. Somehow I'll find some help there.*

Mashhad was far away, a thousand miles. And Javid was leaving the army without permission, which meant he would be thrown into prison if he were caught.

But so many men had been killed, maybe they wouldn't notice that one had just disappeared, especially if he came back before too long. …

Javid hitched rides on trucks and buses and donkeys. Finally, he reached Mashhad and the shrine of the tomb of Imam Reza. Throngs of worshipers, hoping for answers to their prayers, surrounded the tomb, weeping and wailing.

Javid opened his mouth to pray too, but to his surprise, no words would come out. He felt as if his voice were being smothered. *I traveled so far, for days, just to come here to pray, and now I can't pray? What's going on?*

Then he heard a voice coming from somewhere and nowhere. A strong voice, firm, but with a sound of love, like a good father. "Look at this shrine," said the voice. "What do you see?"

Then Javid had words. He muttered, "It's the tomb of a dead man."

The voice spoke again. "Are you asking a dead man to protect your life? Ask Me, for I am your living God. Call upon My Name."

Javid felt as if he should fall down on his face. He looked around to see if anyone else had heard the voice, but it seemed that no one had. Everyone else was still weeping and wailing.

He looked to heaven. "God help me," he prayed simply. "I'm too young to die."

Suddenly, Javid felt desperate to get out of the shrine, away from the tomb of the dead man, away from the wailing worshipers. The thought of an old friend came to mind, a friend who lived in Mashhad.

The friend gladly welcomed the young man and gave him lunch. "Would you like to come with me to a place where we pray?" the friend asked.

"Yes, certainly," answered Javid. "Praying is the reason I came to Mashhad in the first place."

The two drove for an hour and a half. Javid watched out the window and saw that they were driving far out into the countryside. *Where are we going?*

"This is a different kind of prayer," said his friend as they walked into the house.

There were about sixty people gathered, some of them sitting on the floor. "This is Pastor Hossein Soodmand," said the friend. Pastor Soodmand took

Javid in his arms and hugged him as if they were old friends. "Welcome," he said.

"Shh!" said someone. "You left the door open! Close it!"

*Is this a secret meeting?* Javid wondered. *What's going on?*

First, Javid's friend prayed. But it wasn't a memorized prayer. The friend sounded as if he were actually friends with God.

Then the people started singing, with guitars. This was a new thing too!

Then Pastor Soodmand began to preach. He talked about all the trials of life, and how Jesus is the solution to every one. Javid had never heard anything like it before.

Then another prayer. How much these people seemed to love God!

After the meeting, as the people talked with one another, Pastor Soodmand came to Javid. "I understand that you're a soldier," he said. "You've just come from the worst fighting."

"Yes," Javid answered. His eyes darted back and forth. Would Pastor Soodmand know that he had been afraid and ran away? He pulled out a photograph of himself in his uniform. "Yes, I fought in Bosra. All but three in my group were killed."

Pastor Soodmand had tears in his eyes. "My heart breaks for the young men who have been wounded in this

terrible war; not just in their bodies, but in their spirits."
He touched his chest, his heart. "My heart breaks for the
families who have lost loved ones in this terrible war." He
shook his head at the senselessness and horror of it all.

Then Pastor Soodmand took Javid's small photograph in his hand. He put his other hand on Javid's
shoulder. "I tell you, my son. One day you will become
a bold, strong soldier in the army of God."

"What do you mean?" Javid asked. "I don't
understand."

"You'll understand one day," the pastor replied.
"One day, the Lord will tell you what it means. I'll pray
for you through all the days until we meet again." To
his surprise, Javid felt an indescribable peace settle over
him. *Where did that come from?*

That night, Javid stayed with his Christian friend
and heard story after story of how the Living Lord,
Jesus Christ, had shown His power in the lives of the
Christians. "These stories are far greater than the
stories of the Muslim heroes," he pondered.

Soon he returned to Bosra, the place of battle, to the
terrible war that he and all his comrades hated. More
and more and more of them were killed, even young
boys. But Javid was never even hurt.

*"One day, you will become a bold, strong soldier in the army
of God."* Pastor Soodmand's words continued to ring in

Javid's ears. What did he mean? Javid's stomach turned at the thought of killing for God. But he couldn't even imagine that this could be what Pastor Soodmand meant. Not with his kind face and gentle eyes.

He wanted to see Pastor Soodmand again.

How tired, how tired Javid had become of killing, of blood and death and bodies lying all around him. Somehow, though, the peace that he had felt in Mashhad never left him.

Finally, after two terrible years, Javid was allowed to leave the army and go back to Tehran to study. "I just want to put all that behind me and get on with my life," he murmured. Even thoughts of Pastor Soodmand faded away as he studied and worked and dreamed about a good life of wealth and power. That was where he would find peace and happiness.

Wasn't it?

See Thinking Further for Chapter 11 on page 139.

# 12. SOODMAND THE SHADOW (JAVID, PART TWO)

Javid may have been trying to forget Pastor Soodmand, but Pastor Soodmand hadn't forgotten him. Since he often came to meetings in Tehran now, he phoned Javid, again and again, to invite him.

"No, I can't come. I have to study."

"No, I can't come. I'm working late."

"No, I can't come. My schedule is just too full."

Even though Javid still held warm memories of his meeting with Pastor Soodmand, somehow now it seemed that he wanted to think of any excuse to avoid him.

One day, the pastor called him and said, "Look, Javid, tell me how much you earn at your job in a month?"

Javid was surprised. "Why do you want to know?"

"Because I'll pay you that amount to get you to come to one of our meetings."

What kind of a man was this? He just wouldn't stop!

"I'll come," Javid finally said. "You don't have to pay me."

As Javid entered the little apartment, he thought, *Yes, I had warm feelings about that Christian meeting, but how can I endanger all I'm working for? I nearly died in that war, and now I want a good life! I don't want to throw that away for some religion!*

But in that meeting, the prayers and songs and preaching again touched his heart, and Javid found himself struggling in his soul.

After the meeting, Pastor Soodmand came to him. "Javid, I'm going to become your shadow," he announced.

Javid looked at him with quizzical eyes.

"No matter where you go, I'll follow you," the pastor continued. "I'll follow you to your home, to the university, or even to the top of a high mountain. I'll be like your shadow. God has told me not to let you go."

Javid's heart sank. What was he to do? "I'm going home," he said. "You may follow me, if you like."

Pastor Soodmand and two other men from the prayer group went with him.

"Can I fix you some food?" Javid offered politely.

"We'll fix it," said the two men. "You talk with the pastor." They disappeared into the kitchen.

For three hours, Pastor Soodmand talked to Javid about Jesus Christ, the one who loved sinners, the Savior of the world, the glorious King of Kings.

Javid rudely threw out one objection after another.

"How can God have a son?"

"You Christians have three gods!"

"God is too holy to come among men!"

"Jesus did not die on the cross, so He couldn't have risen again!"

On and on, for hours. Gently, kindly, patiently, Pastor Soodmand answered the questions from the Holy Book of the Christians, and continued to emphasize the great love of Jesus Christ, the Shepherd of souls, the only Hope, the Rescuer of mankind.

*How can I be talking this way when I know God protected me during the war?* Javid thought. But still, he persisted.

Finally, at two o'clock in the morning, Javid spewed out, "There's no way I'm going to believe anything about Jesus unless God gives me a sign from heaven!"

"All right, all right, that's good," said the pastor. "That's very good." He shook Javid's hand. "The Lord will do that for you."

Javid continued, "I respect you, but you are deceived by a lie. However," he added, "if I get a sign from heaven, then I'll believe in Jesus Christ as my Lord and God and Master."

Pastor Soodmand opened his Bible to John 20:29. "This is Jesus talking to Thomas," he said. "After Jesus was risen from the dead, Thomas said he wouldn't believe until he saw. Then Jesus appeared to him, and he fell down on his knees and said 'My Lord and my God.' Jesus said, 'Thomas, because you have seen me, you have believed. Blessed are those who have not seen and yet have believed.' "

Pastor Soodmand continued to talk and turn to other Bible verses. But Javid didn't hear him.

Instead, Javid heard a different voice. It was the same voice he had heard two years earlier when he visited the shrine in the city of Mashhad. "Javid! Javid!" the voice called, strong and firm, yet gentle, like a loving father. "Are you trying to test Me, or am I the One who must test you? I am the Lord. Don't try to take authority that belongs only to Me."

Javid felt himself alone someplace far away from that couch where Pastor Soodmand was still speaking with gentleness and urgency. He felt surrounded by the holiness of God and then suddenly overwhelmed by his sin. Every sin he had ever committed seemed to cover him like leprosy.

*My life! I give my life to You! Save me from my sin!* It was a feeling more than a thought.

But suddenly he came back to the present, to the physical world, to the couch where Pastor Soodmand continued to talk. How much time had passed? Only moments. But somehow, it seemed like an eternity.

"I believe!" Javid cried out. "I believe in Jesus Christ with my whole heart!" He suddenly realized that both of his hands were lifted high.

Pastor Soodmand began to leap in the air and shout praises. "Hallelujah!" he cried. "Hallelujah! I knew you would become one of the soldiers in the army of God!"

The two men came from the kitchen.

"Do you have any idea what just happened?" Javid asked.

"Of course we do!" they said. "It doesn't take four hours to fix something to eat! We've been praying for you in there, the whole time!"

"Javid," said Pastor Soodmand, "God has something very important for you to do, but I'm not sure what it is. He'll show you in His time."

In time, God showed Javid that He had called him to be an evangelist. Many, many people came to Christ through his bold and fervent witness.

One day, Javid saw a young woman studying at the library. Something in his spirit drew him to her. "Lord, what are you saying to me?" he murmured. "She's obviously a Muslim, and I don't want to marry a Muslim. I want to marry a Christian."

But the Holy Spirit of God pressed this young woman on his heart again and again and again. Finally Javid asked her father for her hand in marriage. *She's young, so maybe she'll be open to discussing spiritual things,* he thought.

He became engaged to Mina. And then he went to his regular Monday night prayer group. ...

And all the people rejoiced together to see what God had done.

\* \* \*

Not long after Mina and Javid's marriage, Mina's faithful friend Monir was arrested, tortured, and killed for her Christianity. Mina and Javid's faith was discovered, and they had to run for their lives. Mina's father, who had loved her so much, shouted at her over the phone, "I have erased every memory of you from our home and identity cards. You no longer exist, you ungrateful girl."

Mina and Javid went on to establish Touch of Christ Ministries. Through the years, as they worked for the Lord in Spain, Holland, and the United States, they saw Him work many miracles. In Mina's mind, though, the greatest miracle of all came twenty years later when she received a phone call from her father. He too had received a miraculous vision of Jesus Christ. He and his wife, Mina's mother, had both become joyful believers in the one true Savior of their souls.

See Thinking Further for Chapter 12 on page 140.

# 13. BLOOD OF THE MARTYRS, SEED OF THE CHURCH (HAIK, RASHIN)

**P**astor Soodmand was dead! He had been killed by the Iranian police, who said he was a criminal for becoming a Christian and evangelizing.

They had warned him, they said. They had warned him to stop. But he just wouldn't stop talking about Jesus. Anyone who left the holy religion of Islam deserved to die!

But he knew he couldn't stop giving the Living Water to those around him. So in 1990, he became a martyr for the Savior he loved.

After the Soodmand family found out the shocking news, their friend Pastor Haik Hovsepian gathered together with them and some others to give them comfort. There was Hossein Soodmand's widow. There were the four young children. Rashin, the older daughter, was just thirteen years old. All of them were wiping their eyes.

"Listen to me, my friends," said Haik. "Sometimes God uses death to show us more important realities.

For our Brother Soodmond, I know that death was just a short walk from this world to the other. I began to see the picture of heaven more clearly. God allows us to be persecuted—even to become martyrs—so that we'll know for sure that the spiritual world is more real than the physical world."

But some of the Christians became afraid. One of their pastors had been murdered! What would happen to all the rest of them?

"We won't fight!" said Pastor Haik. "Those who live by the sword will die by the sword. God Himself will be the one to take revenge on those who harm His people."

But that didn't stop Haik from speaking out. He wrote letters to people and spoke publicly about how wrong it was to murder a pastor who was only good, who had hurt no one, and who left behind a blind wife and four children. Haik helped to care for that widow and those children, just like Jesus. The Iranian government saw this, and they were angry.

Haik Hovsepian had made them angry before, too. He had been preaching and helping all the churches throughout the country. In the 1980s, he had become the superintendent of all the Protestant churches in Iran. Certainly the government noticed him.

"New restrictions for Christians!" the government ordered. "You can't conduct your Christian meetings in the Persian language. Every single person who comes to your meetings, you have to report to the government. We have to approve all your church members."

"Absolutely not!" said Haik. "Our churches are open to anyone who wants to come." After all, every Iranian should have the right to follow Jesus Christ as his Lord and Savior.

More and more secret meetings sprang up all over Iran throughout the early 1990s. Haik visited the small churches and encouraged them.

But in 1993, Haik spoke out to all the nations of the world. "Another pastor has been arrested, and they say they'll kill him!" he proclaimed to national leaders. "Write letters to the government of Iran and tell them that they need to let him go!"

Thousands of Christians did. The Iranian government did let that pastor go, but they were angry, very angry. The Christians cheered and praised God, but they wondered if the Iranian government was planning something sinister.

Three days later, Haik Hovsepian himself was taken and killed.

This time, the news spread not just through the churches of Iran, but through churches all over the world. Haik Hovsepian, the good man who had helped so many, had been murdered. He had been martyred for his Savior!

Even Christians from other countries came to that funeral. Thousands of people from all over the world wrote letters to Haik's family. "We stand with you! We thank God for your husband's brave life and sacrificial death! We're praying for you and your family!"

Christians of Iran became braver. They attended the funeral and even videotaped it. They knew that government officials would probably steal their videotapes and threaten them, but that didn't stop the Christians from coming. They wanted to show their support for their brave martyr pastors. They wanted to show their love for the Lord. They wanted to show that they, too, would stand for Jesus Christ.

The next Sunday, in churches all over Iran, pastors said, "We know that we may be next. We may be killed for our faith in Christ. But, by the power of the Holy Spirit, we'll continue to love and stand strong on the solid Rock of Jesus Christ."

Christians wrote letters and signed their names with their own blood. "We're ready to stand together in Christ till the very end. We're ready to give our lives."

One pastor preached, "Where the blood of the saints has fallen, there the church of the saints will grow! A church that is not afraid of death will never be defeated!"

And sure enough, more pastors were killed. But that didn't stop the Church of Jesus Christ in Iran. More and more Muslims came to these Christians, whispering, "How is Christianity so strong that you're willing to peacefully give up your lives for it? I want something that real!"

More and more of the young people of Iran became willing to give their lives. Haik's widow and four children moved to the United States to start Hovsepian Ministries. Through it, they produce satellite programs that are broadcast to millions of Iranian people. People who meet in the secret churches are being encouraged in their faith, and many Muslims are coming to Christ.

\* \* \*

In 1990, thirteen-year-old Rashin Soodmand wondered how she could go on living after her beloved father, Hossein Soodmand, had been killed. But she knew God was calling her to be an evangelist like him.

"How can we do it?" she asked her friends. "We can't get any New Testaments or pamphlets. The government is destroying them all." The friends prayed together.

"Let's write out Scriptures on paper," one friend suggested. "We'll leave them around the city."

So, with their one precious Bible, they did just that. Late at night, after school, Rashin and her friends spent hours copying out Bible verses onto pieces of paper. Then, during the day, they left the papers here and there around the city of Mashhad—on restaurant tables, in restrooms, in shops, and taxis. Sometimes, when the Holy Spirit led them, they even put the papers directly into the hands of strangers.

*The single verses are good*, thought Rashin. *But I want to do something more.*

She decided to write out the entire Gospel of John. Every night after school, late at night, she copied a whole chapter into a little notebook.

When the notebook was finally finished, she carefully wrapped it in wrapping paper, like a gift. Then she went walking. "Lord God, Holy Spirit, show me where you want me to leave this precious gift," she said.

There was one house, next to all the others, looking not that much different. But her heart felt peace. She left it there.

Rashin still doesn't know how God used that Gospel of John. But years later, she went to England to study with Elam Ministries and an old friend of her father's, Sam Yeghnazar. "Please God, we need more Bibles for the Muslim people," she prayed.

She stayed on with Elam after her studies, and began to teach the Bible over satellite. Thousands — even millions — of Iranians have listened to her gentle voice and true words.

By 2013, Rashin was able to report, "There are now more than one million New Testaments in the hands of the Iranian people. Pray for the second million. The Iranian people already believe that Jesus is a prophet. They love finding out more about Him."

See Thinking Further for Chapter 13 on page 140.

# 14. THE IMAM WORSHIPER (PADINA, PART ONE)

ighteen-year-old Padina gasped. There was a hole in her black stocking! A hole as big as a coin! Surely someone could see her ankle!

She ran back inside the House of Zeinab from her sweeping, heaving and sobbing with terror. If anyone had seen her ankle, then in heaven Allah could treat her like a yo-yo, sending her down to hell to burn her feet and ankles and legs, over and over and over.

Desperately Padina rummaged through her things, looking for an intact stocking. "I didn't do it on purpose!" she whispered through her chattering teeth. "I'm trying to do everything right!" Oh, how desperately she wanted to do everything right.

"I can see a little bit of your hair sticking out from your scarf!" hissed one of the other girls. "You could burn in hell forever! Or Allah will hang you from your hair."

Padina began shaking back and forth and holding herself with her arms. "I didn't mean to!" she whispered. "I didn't mean to!"

When she was only a child, Padina had started reciting prayers for six hours every night in order to please Allah. She wanted so much to enter paradise. She wanted so much to have peace.

But in the middle of her prayers, her heart would pound. *Did I wash correctly? If I haven't washed correctly, my prayers will only anger Allah, not please him!* Again and again through the night, every night, she stopped to wash again, hoping this time she was doing it right.

When she was fourteen, Padina had begun her studies at the House of Zeinab every day after school. This special school for women taught her how to study the Koran, and how to worship the imams, the men of Allah of long ago. This would be true holiness, the teachers said, and would give peace.

Now, with fresh stockings on, and properly covered from head to toe, Padina entered the small room where the pictures of the twelve holy imams looked down at her sternly. "Please tell Allah I didn't mean to do it," she whispered. "Please tell him that I am wholly devoted to him, and to you." For hours she stayed in that room, praying for each of the holy imams and all their family members.

It was Tuesday. That meant that four hundred women of all ages would arrive from around the area to pray and sing for the dead. Padina led the singing. They sang for Imam Hussain, Zeinab's brother, who had died in battle so long ago.

"O Father Hussain

O father of all the oppressed, Hussain

Why are you dead? Why have they killed you?

Without you, I will perish, O Hussain.

After all, in you are all my hopes!"

*Louder, louder!* thought Padina. *I want to be sure he hears me!*

Every birthday of each of the twelve imams was celebrated with songs of grieving and many tears. But the celebration of the deaths meant even more mourning. Day after day, mourning and weeping and wailing and sobbing. Twelve births and twelve deaths, twenty-four times a year.

Men lined the streets for the Parade of Grief for the death of the Imam Reza. The Ayatollah Khomeini had made a law that no singing would be allowed at a death parade, so they shouted in their grief instead, swaying back and forth, marching in long lines, hoping Allah and the imams would notice them and grant them their requests. They beat themselves with chains until they turned black and blue. Some of them stained their white robes red with their own blood.

Padina watched at the window, hidden behind the dark curtain. She wished she could march in the parade. Surely if she were a man, Allah and the imams would notice her and smile upon her. But she was only a woman. A woman who got a hole in her stocking. Padina shuddered and turned inside towards the others.

She formed a circle with the women. They swayed back and forth like the men, weeping and wailing. They scratched their faces till they bled, pulling out their hair, beating their heads on the floor.

*I can't cry enough*, Padina thought. *Mohammed's daughter feared Allah so much that she cried a whole pot full of tears! I could never cry that much. No matter how much I cry, I can't cry enough to please Allah.* But still, every night she collected all her tears, hoping that when Allah saw them, he would say they were enough.

Night after night she woke up in a cold sweat with another nightmare. Falling, falling under the earth, where all the spirits of the dead attacked her, because she wasn't good enough. Never, never, never enough!

When Padina was twenty-one she gave up. Living in the House of Zeinab had brought her no peace. By the end of that time, her anguish was worse than ever. The god she had tried to love and please was a god she had learned only to fear and dread.

Padina became an ordinary Muslim, like most of the other people of Iran. She said her memorized prayers five times a day and worked a regular job. She married. But no matter how hard she tried to be a good wife, her husband was still cruel and unfaithful. As time passed, she began to sink into depression.

One night after dinner, Padina flopped down on the couch alone and turned on the television. She saw something she had never seen before.

"Jesus is my light! Jesus is my light!" the people on stage sang.

Then the camera turned to show many other people, singing and clapping their hands.

*They all look so happy,* Padina thought. *They're not weeping and wailing!* All the Muslim holy men looked angry all the time. These people looked peaceful and joyful.

There had been no freedom in the House of Zeinab. But somehow there seemed to be freedom here. *I want to be happy like them!* Padina bit her lip to keep from sobbing.

The next night, Padina again secretly watched that program, *Iran Alive!* A phone number came on the screen.

"I'm going to do it. I'm going to call them," she said.

"Hello? Welcome!" said the man on the screen.

"I want to speak to the man with the white hair," Padina said. "Hormoz."

"Yes?" said Pastor Hormoz Shariat, smiling. "How can I help you?"

"I want to know why you all are so happy," said Padina.

"I'm so glad you asked that question!" Pastor Hormoz answered. "It's because of Jesus Christ! He has taken all the punishment for our sins! He rose again from the dead so that we can have victory over our sins through faith in Him!"

Padina didn't really understand. But somehow it sounded beautiful.

Every night, month after month, Padina secretly watched *Iran Alive!* She loved seeing the happy people and was curious to hear them talk about Jesus. They seemed so full of love, like she had never seen before anywhere.

But how could they say that the prophet, Jesus, was actually God? She turned the channel in disgust. *Filthy infidels, to think that a man was God.*

See Thinking Further for Chapter 14 on page 141.

# 15. IRAN ALIVE!
## (PADINA, PART TWO)

Somehow, Padina got a copy of the Persian New Testament and began to read it secretly. She often called the *Iran Alive!* program and asked that gentle man, Pastor Hormoz, her many questions. Her voice carried over the phone line to be broadcast to millions of Iranians, watching and listening. She listened to Pastor Hormoz answer her over the television screen.

One night when she called, he recognized her voice.

"Padina," said Pastor Hormoz, "I want to ask you a question. Who is Jesus Christ to you?"

*He called me by my first name, like a friend.* Padina was surprised. "Who is Jesus Christ to me?" She had never put it into words before.

She remembered the very first night she had turned on the program. "Jesus is my light," they had sung. The House of Zeinab had been a world of darkness.

Padina felt her voice catch in her throat.

"I see Jesus as someone who is Light," she said hesitantly. "He's the Light of God, who has been divided off from God."

Pastor Hormoz replied, "Jesus says in the Bible that He is the Light of the World. He says that whoever follows Him will not walk in darkness, but will have the light of life." Then he said, "Padina, may I pray for you?"

Padina's eyes filled with tears as she watched Pastor Hormoz on the screen. She could barely answer. "Yes."

As he prayed, something softened in her heart. *Jesus is more,* she thought. *Jesus is more than a prophet. He's more than an imam. He's more.*

Then the worst possible things happened. Not only was Padina's mother diagnosed with a terrible deadly disease, but her husband told her he was going to divorce her. There was no greater shame for a Muslim woman. One night, Padina decided to use a handful of her depression pills to take her life. She urged her mother to do the same.

But just then her mother turned on *Iran Alive!*

"Are you taking medication for depression?" Pastor Hormoz was asking. "Are you thinking about killing yourself?" Padina and her mother both gasped and looked at each other. How did he know?

"The Lord says, 'stop,'" Pastor Hormoz said. "He has a hope and a future for you. Stop and call me."

Immediately Padina's mother reached over from the couch and picked up the phone to call Pastor Hormoz.

"I'm going to do this!" Padina shouted, shaking her fist full of pills at her mother. "You can't stop me!"

Padina's mother cried and prayed with Pastor Hormoz over the phone line that was heard by millions of viewers on the television screen. She prayed to Jesus, asking Him to save her. Then she held out the phone to Padina. "Please talk to him," she begged.

"No, you have become an infidel!" Padina shouted. "Why did you do this in the last days of your life? Now you will go to hell for sure!"

"Please, Padina," her mother begged again.

"No! Jesus can do nothing for me! He is nothing!"

Padina's mother kept weeping and begging. Finally, in her anger, Padina grabbed the phone and spoke right to Pastor Hormoz. "Your Jesus can do nothing for me. No one cares about me! My husband is divorcing me! I live a cursed life!"

"Padina," Pastor Hormoz's voice came over the phone, and over the screen. It sounded so kind. "Don't you know that you're valuable to God?"

His gentle tone broke the hardness in Padina's heart, and she began to cry. "I tried for seven years to get

Allah to love me," she sobbed. "I tried for ten years to get my husband to love me. It's no use trying any more!"

Pastor Hormoz's face shone with light and love. "God loves you! You're valuable to Him!" he said. "Don't you see that Jesus wants to save you from all that?"

"No, I don't!" Padina suddenly felt angry again. "He can't do anything for me!"

"You say you tried for seven years to get Allah to love you?"

"Yes! I kept every rule, but I could never keep them enough!"

"And you tried for ten years to get your husband to love you?"

"Yes! Even when he was unfaithful, I always took him back! But now, this is the greatest shame."

"So you've tried everything in your religion."

"Yes, and Jesus can't save me. He can't stop me from doing this."

"All right," said Pastor Hormoz gently. "You're going to take all those pills, and I can't do anything to stop you. But will you try one thing first?" Before she could reply, he continued. "Take just a few days, just a week, to do something. Here's what I want you to do. I'm going to show you how you can know Jesus personally—"

*Know Him personally?* She rolled her eyes.

"Spend the next week walking with my Lord Jesus. If He doesn't help your depression in that time, then go kill yourself."

Padina's heart was hard. *This is the way I'll finally please Allah,* she thought. *I'll trick this infidel preacher. I'll agree to follow Jesus for a week. Then, in a week, I'll come back on this program and take all these pills right here on the air, while I'm on the phone with this man. I'll show everyone that Christianity is meaningless and Jesus can do nothing. Then I can say to Allah, "Even killing myself was for you."*

Pastor Hormoz was still speaking. "You'll see," he said. "Jesus will make a difference in your life." Then he began to pray again.

As always, when he prayed, Padina knew that he was talking to someone real, someone who was right there in the room, someone he loved. His voice sounded . . . it sounded like he was crying, weeping for Padina.

"Padina, will you pray a prayer with me?" he asked.

Padina could hardly keep herself from sobbing. "Yes."

She repeated the prayer after him. "Jesus, I repent of my sins. Come into my life. I want to walk with You."

She hung up the phone and looked at her mother. She had done it. Let the challenge begin.

But somehow, something seemed different.

The next morning, Padina could hardly believe her eyes. There came her mother, walking down the hallway.

"Mother, you shouldn't be walking without my help!" she cried. "You should be in bed!"

"Padina," said her mother. "I'm well. The disease has left my body."

Padina felt a sense of panic. "No, it hasn't! You're imagining it! We need to get you to the hospital right away!"

At the hospital, the doctors examined Padina's mother for hours, with different tests and questions. Finally, one of the doctors spoke to Padina. "This is a miracle," he said. "The disease is completely gone."

Then he asked, "Which imam did you pray to?"

Memories of her years of prayer to the imams flooded Padina's mind. She paused before answering to think about her words.

"It wasn't an imam," she said. "We didn't pray to an imam. We prayed to Jesus."

As soon as she said those words, Padina's heart was filled with joy, and she wanted to burst with praise.

She and her mother left the hospital and praised Jesus together. "Jesus, You are the Living God!" Padina cried. "You have cleansed me and filled me! I'll give up my life for You!"

The dark cloud of depression lifted. She began to read the Bible again, with an open heart. By a miraculous work, Jesus delivered her of her depression, anger, hatred, and bitterness.

Every Thursday night, Padina and her mother invited different people over for dinner. After dinner they would sit around sipping tea, and one of them would turn on the TV. As they would hear the familiar *Iran Alive!* theme music, they would say to their guests, "Oh, what a nice looking program. What do you suppose it is?"

All the visitors would immediately become interested. They listened to Pastor Hormoz and began to be amazed by the love of Jesus Christ. When the tears began to glisten in their eyes, Padina would say, "Why don't you call in? Ask him your questions."

They did. And many of them came to Christ. And at the end of the phone call, they would say to Pastor Hormoz, "By the way, Padina says hello."

"Give our warm greetings to Padina," Pastor Hormoz would answer. "She took a step toward God in faith, and He proved Himself faithful."

See Thinking Further for Chapter 15 on page 141.

# 16. A MAN ON A DONKEY (TAHER)

Taher stumbled from room to room. They were gone. All of them. All of them were gone.

His daughter. She had turned first. There was her Koran, on the little table by her bed. That cursed Bible? Surely she had taken that with her.

His wife—she held the coveted title of Hajieh—a woman who had made the pilgrimage to holy Mecca! But she had turned to this accursed Christianity too. There was her head covering, lying on the floor.

His son. He had turned last. That was when Taher had started beating them all, threatening to kill them, frantic to force them to turn away from this devilish religion. But they had only pleaded with him and prayed for him.

There was a note. "We love you, Papa, but we have to escape. We're praying for you."

*How can it be? How can they all be gone?* Taher pounded his fist on the wall. *No!* He found a vase, and with great fury, threw it across the room. The splintering shatters seemed to echo again and again.

Then he sat down on the bed and sobbed. They were gone.

Day after day, Taher came home from work to an empty house. He asked everyone, but no one knew where they had gone. More and more he felt in a fog of grief and despair. He turned to the Koran.

"Obey Allah and His Messenger" read the Koran, "… be patient and persevering: for Allah is with those who patiently persevere."

"Allah is with those who patiently persevere," Taher repeated. "I'll patiently persevere." Day after day he went to work and came home, said his prayers and memorized the Koran. He hoped and prayed for word from his family. But no word came.

"Seek his help with patient perseverance and prayer," read the Koran, "it is indeed hard, except to those who bring a lowly spirit."

"My spirit is very low," said Taher. "Very, very low."

"O you who believe!" read the Koran. "Do your duty to Allah and fear him. And seek the way to approach him, and strive hard in his cause so that you may be successful."

"Haven't I strived?" Taher cried out. "Am I not a Haji? I made the pilgrimage to Mecca! Don't I give alms? I do all the prayers and the fasts! I believe in the sinlessness of Mohammed and Fatimeh and the imams! I even memorize the Koran!" He walked around his house, from one empty room to another. "What kind of success is this?" he cried to the empty rooms.

Taher fell face down on the floor, his shoulders heaving with sobs. "Please, Allah, show me your face! My family talked about a God who revealed Himself to them. But you are the true God! Reveal yourself to me!"

As day after day passed in darkness and silence, the first small feelings of doubt began to bubble up in his heart.

Jesus? The Bible? It was unthinkable!

"Where are you?!" he cried.

But finally one night, sobbing in his bed, Taher moaned, "I'll believe in the God who reveals Himself to me."

The Living God answered his prayer.

That night, asleep in his bed, in the darkness of his room, Taher saw a man on a donkey coming toward him. Who was he? Where was he coming from?

The man got off the donkey and reached out. "I'll cleanse you from all your sins," He said. Then He hugged Taher. "You're free. I'll give you rest. Believe in Me."

Taher fell down on his knees. "What will happen if I sin again?" he asked.

The man climbed back onto his donkey and rode away. His last words were, "I'll cleanse you from all your sins."

Taher stood gazing after the strange man. Who was He? What did He mean?

Then in his vision another man came. "Do you know who that man on the donkey is?" he asked.

"No," said Taher.

"He is Jesus Christ. He'll cleanse you from your sins." And that man too disappeared.

Then Taher woke up.

What could it mean? How could a prophet cleanse anyone from his sins?

Maybe that dream was from the devil. Taher tried to go back to sleep.

In his fitful sleep, he had the same dream again. The man on the donkey came. He said the same words. He left. Then the other man came. "Do you know who that man on the donkey is? He is Jesus Christ. He will cleanse you from your sins."

This time when Taher woke up, he was shaking. How could he have this same dream twice? He was a faithful Muslim! He had been a faithful Muslim from his earliest memories. He had made the pilgrimage to Mecca—he was a Haji! What was this dream—was it telling him to leave Islam? Unthinkable!

Finally, after tossing and turning, he fell asleep again.

And there He was again—the man on the donkey. The kindness in His eyes. The hug! "I will cleanse you from your sins."

"Do you know who that man is? He is Jesus Christ! He will cleanse you from your sins."

Taher sat bolt upright in bed. Three times! He had had the same dream three times!

"Who are you?" he called to the darkness. "Where are you?"

Then he cried out, almost against his will, "Jesus Christ!" He gripped the bedclothes, shaking. He couldn't say the words yet, but the thought was in his mind. *Jesus Christ is the only true God.*

Taher climbed out of bed, feeling like a different person. *Jesus Christ is true. That means that Islam is false. I need help. What should I do?*

He had to get to the Christian church. The only church he knew about was the church he had told his family they could never attend. But he needed help—he needed to find out more about this man on the donkey.

The next Friday, when the Christian house church was meeting, Taher cautiously approached the door. When a man walked inside, Taher slipped in behind him. There were the Christians, sitting in a circle in the small room.

"It's Taher!" people whispered to each other. "Why is he here?"

The Christians had all been praying for Taher for over a year. Some of them had helped Taher's family escape the country. They knew how much he hated Christianity, and how he had beaten his family and even threatened to kill them.

So why was he here? Would he turn them all in to the secret police, the way he had told his family he would do?

A church leader came up to him. "How can I help you?" he asked politely.

Taher looked down and then looked around. At first, he didn't know what to say. "I want to pray," he stammered. "I want to go to church." He hesitated again. "I want to give my life to Christ. I need help, because I don't know how to do that."

The church leader's eyes grew large. Everyone turned to look, and no one said a word.

Taher spoke again, and this time he spoke to the whole group. "I saw Jesus in a dream!" he said. "I saw him face to face! He said He would cleanse me from my sins!" His voice choked in his throat.

Then he walked in and sat down quietly in the group. He closed his eyes to listen to the singing about the love of Christ, who had died to cleanse us from all our sins, who had risen to give us freedom. "You will give me rest," he murmured. "I will believe in You."

\* \* \*

Taher grew in the Christian faith quickly, with great love and power in the Holy Spirit. After drinking long and deep of the Living Water, he became like a river to those around him, risking his life for Jesus.

One day, Taher was able to escape Iran and join his family in another country. Together they rejoiced in the great salvation of the One who cleanses from sins and makes us free. Together they're praying for the people of Iran to find this great freedom and know this great love.

See Thinking Further for Chapter 16 on page 142.

# 17. LIVING WATER IN THE DESERT

In 1979, when the Ayatollah came into power in Iran, there were about four hundred Muslim-background believers (MBBs) in the country.

Later, even the president of Iran himself admitted that about four hundred Muslims were turning to Christ *every single month*. Some people think it's far more than this.

More Muslims in Iran have come to Christ in the last thirty or forty years than in the thirteen hundred years that Islam has been in the country.

Persecution is continuing. Pastor Saeed Abedini, who also came to Christ from a Muslim background, through a dream and other great works of God, was arrested in 2012 for evangelizing. His wife, Naghmeh, began to travel the world speaking on his behalf, taking every opportunity she could to tell people who Jesus Christ is and what He can do for hungry, thirsty souls. Many more Iranians are listening.

And more and more and more are coming to Christ.

The Living Water has been sprinkling on the land, then pouring, then gushing like a river that cannot be stopped. The thirsty people of Iran are drinking of the Living Water of Jesus Christ.

See Thinking Further for Chapter 17 on page 142.

# A MESSAGE FROM THE AUTHOR

For years I've been hearing that a great movement of God was going on in Iran, similar to the movement we had heard about in China decades ago. Finally, when I began to research, I found story after story, with the majority of them published within the last ten years.

As I love to do, I did my best to trace the stories back to the source—where had this person heard the gospel, and then, where had *that* person heard the gospel? I watched the finger of God tracing a pattern throughout the country—the faithfulness of a few who were called, and took that precious gift to the hands of some, who carried it to the hands of others, who watched it, like the bread Jesus blessed in John 6, multiply more and more and more. Like the river Ezekiel passed over, we have the privilege of watching the trickling stream that flowed from their innermost beings (John 7:38) become a mighty flood for the glory of God. And we stand humbled and amazed at His great work.

# ABOUT THE MISSIONARIES AND THE IRANIAN CHRISTIANS

*Chapter 1 "A Hard, Dry Land"*

Henry Martyn was a missionary to the Near East, who succeeded in translating the New Testament into three different languages before he died of a fever at the age of thirty-one in 1812.

*Chapter 2 "Kurds and the Way"*

Justin Perkins was the first missionary from the United States to Persia (which was later called Iran). His book *Missionary Life in Persia* provides much insight into the world of the Persians through the eyes of an American. Saeed's story is told in *The Beloved Physician of Teheran*, by Isaac Yonan.

*Chapter 3 "Wild Woman in the Desert"*

Mary Bird was a missionary in Isfahan, Persia, from 1891 until her death in 1914. Her story is found in several books, including *She Went Alone: Mary Bird of Persia*, by Constance Savery.

*Chapters 4 and 6 "The Only Prophet That's True" and "Stone the Victorious One"*
Rajab's and Hasan's stories are found in *Ten Muslims Meet Christ,* by William Miller. I wasn't able to discover the identity of the influential missionary in Rajab's story, but Benjamin Badal in chapter 6 was a highly respected missionary from western Iran, of Assyrian descent, trained by Justin Perkins.

*Chapter 5 "Sowing Seed in a Desert Place"*
William Miller served Christ in Persia from 1919 until 1962. His stories are recounted in *My Persian Pilgrimage* and *Tales from Persia.*

*Chapters 7 and 8 "Christian Dogs" and "Arise and Eat!"*
Hossein Soodmand's story is recounted on the Elam Ministries website.

*Chapters 9-12 "The Mysterious Book," "Who Is That Young Man?," "The Reluctant Soldier," and "Soodmand the Shadow"*
Mina Nevisa tells her story, and the story of her husband, Javid, in *Miracle of Miracles,* which you can obtain directly from them at Touch of Christ Ministries, P.O. Box 223492, Chantilly, VA 20153, or from their website at www.touchofchrist.net.

*Chapter 13 "Blood of the Martyrs, Seed of the Church"*
The story of the martyrs, especially Haik Hovsepian, is told in the video *A Cry from Iran,* produced by Hovsepian Ministries.

Sam Yeghnazar is a zealous and passionate Armenian Christian whose family did much to spread the gospel in Iran. He eventually left his home country and set up Elam Ministries in England, a ministry that reaches Iranians for Christ through the internet.

The story of Rahin Soodmand is told on the Elam Ministries website.

*Chapters 14 and 15 "The Imam Worshiper"* and *"Iran Alive!"*
Padina's story is told in the book *Iran: Desperate for God,* published by Voice of the Martyrs. A re-enacted version of it is also available on Youtube.

Hormoz Shariat has hosted the *Iran Alive!* satellite program since 2001, answering the questions of seeking Muslims, and seeing thousands of them turn to Jesus Christ for salvation.

*Chapter 16 "A Man on a Donkey"*
Taher's story is told on the Open Doors website, the website of Brother Andrew, the Bible smuggler, at www.opendoorsusa.org. The original story is called "A Modern Day Paul in Iran."

## Chapter 17 "Living Water in the Desert"

Saeed Abedini's story is told many places on the internet. You can watch videos of his wife Naghmeh speaking in churches all over the world, passionately telling their story and speaking of the love and power of Jesus Christ.

# THINKING FURTHER

## CHAPTER 1 - A HARD, DRY LAND

*How beautiful upon the mountains are the feet of him who brings good news, who publishes peace, who brings good news of happiness, who publishes salvation, who says to Zion, "Your God reigns"* (Isaiah 52:7).

What was the earlier name of the land of Iran?

How long ago did the gospel first come to the land of Iran?

Why do you think people didn't want to accept it?

## CHAPTER 2 - KURDS AND THE WAY

*[Jesus said,] "By this all people will know that you are my disciples, if you have love for one another"* (John 13:35).

An "infidel" is someone who leaves the true faith. What faith did the Kurds think was the true faith? Why do you think they would want to kill someone who left it?

The Koran, the holy book of the Muslims, tells Muslims to respect "People of the Book." Why do you think Saeed didn't obey that rule?

What did Saeed see in Pastor Yohannan that seemed better than his own life?

Why did Saeed put burning coals on his legs?

What did God do for Saeed when he cried out to Him?

## CHAPTER 3 – WILD WOMAN IN THE DESERT

*And [Jesus] went throughout all Galilee, preaching in their synagogues and casting out demons (Mark 1:39).*

Why was Mary Bird such an important worker in Persia?

Why was the woman chained up outside of town?

What did Mary do for the woman that helped her become calm?

What made the woman think that Christianity must be true?

## CHAPTER 4 – THE ONLY PROPHET THAT'S TRUE

*And Jesus went throughout all the cities and villages, teaching in their synagogues and proclaiming the gospel of the kingdom and healing every disease and every affliction (Matthew 9:35).*

What did the teacher say that disturbed Rajab so much?

What made Rajab finally decide that the Koran was full of confusion?

What made Rajab's life become so dark and hopeless?

Why did he decide to seek out the missionary and ask him questions?

What did the missionary tell him about sin?

What did Rajab find out when he read the New Testament?

What did his new name mean?

## CHAPTER 5 – SOWING SEED IN A DESERT PLACE

*And as Moses lifted up the serpent in the wilderness, so must the Son of Man be lifted up, that whoever believes in him may have eternal life (John 3:14-15).*

Why did William Miller grow out his red beard?

What made William think he was a failure when he left Seistan the first time?

How many years went by before William was able to return to that area?

How had the chief become a Christian?

Why was it a surprise to William?

## CHAPTER 6 – STONE THE VICTORIOUS ONE

*He [Jesus] said to them, "But who do you say that I am?" Simon Peter replied, "You are the Christ, the Son of the living God (Matthew 16:15-16).*

What unkind trick did Hasan and his friends play on the camels and the people?

Why did Hasan reject the Muslim religion?

Why did he reject the Baha'i religion?

Hasan couldn't read. How did he learn the Gospel of Matthew?

What did his new name mean?

What did Mansur do for the next sixteen years of his life?

# CHAPTER 7 – CHRISTIAN DOGS

*Jesus said to them, "I am the bread of life; whoever comes to me shall not hunger, and whoever believes in me shall never thirst" (John 6:35).*

What did Hossein's uncle teach him when he was little?

How did he show that he hated the Christians when he was a boy?

How did the Christian woman and his Christian friend in the army both surprise him?

What did the voice tell Hossein in his dream?

After Hossein became a Christian, what was he afraid would happen in his family?

# CHAPTER 8 – ARISE AND EAT!

*[Jesus said] "I am the living bread that came down from heaven. If anyone eats of this bread, he will live forever. And the bread that I will give for the life of the world is my flesh" (John 6:51).*

The religion of Islam says that Jesus Christ is one of the prophets. Why was Hossein's uncle angry about Hossein believing in Him?

Why did Hossein have to leave home?

How did the Iranian Revolution change the way mission work was done in Iran?

Why did Hossein go back to Mashhad, his home city?

## CHAPTER 9 – THE MYSTERIOUS BOOK

*Jesus said to him, "I am the way, and the truth, and the life. No one comes to the Father except through me" (John 14:6).*

Why were Mina's father and brother-in-law so angry with her?

Why was her father's reaction so confusing to Mina?

What did Mina see about Jesus that was different from Mohammed?

What made Mina think that there must be some Christians in Iran?

How did Monir find out about Jesus?

## CHAPTER 10 – WHO IS THAT YOUNG MAN?

*And it shall come to pass that everyone who calls upon the name of the Lord shall be saved (Acts 2:21).*

Why was Mina excited about meeting pastor Hossein Soodmand?

What happened to her at that meeting that she had been praying for, for years?

Describe how Mina and Javid got engaged.

What surprised Mina when she went to the Monday night meeting instead of the Thursday night meeting?

## CHAPTER 11 – THE RELUCTANT SOLDIER

*My soul thirsts for God, for the living God. When shall I come and appear before God? (Psalm 42:2).*

Why did Javid want to go to Mashhad?

What happened there that was frustrating to him? What happened that was surprising?

How did Pastor Soodmand show his love for Javid?

What did Pastor Soodmand tell Javid he would become? What do you think he meant?

## CHAPTER 12 – SOODMAND THE SHADOW

*Jesus said to him, "Have you believed because you have seen me? Blessed are those who have not seen and yet have believed"* (John 20:29).

Why didn't Javid want to come to the meeting of the Christians?

What did Pastor Soodmand mean when he said he was going to become Javid's shadow?

What did Javid say needed to happen for him to become a Christian?

How did God do that?

## CHAPTER 13 – BLOOD OF THE MARTYRS, SEED OF THE CHURCH

*And they have conquered [the enemy] by the blood of the Lamb and by the word of their testimony, for they loved not their lives even unto death* (Revelation 12:11).

Why was Pastor Soodmand killed?

How did Haik Hovsepian set an example for other Christians in Iran?

How did Christianity in Iran change during this period?

How did Rashin Soodmand become an evangelist when she was only a teenage girl?

## CHAPTER 14 – THE IMAM WORSHIPER

*The people dwelling in darkness have seen a great light, and for those dwelling in the region and shadow of death, on them a light has dawned (Matthew 4:16).*

When Padina studied at the House of Zeinab, why was she so afraid all the time?

What were some of the terrible things the people had to do to try to get their god to hear them?

Why did Padina quit studying at the House of Zeinab?

What attracted Padina about the television program *Iran Alive!*?

## CHAPTER 15 – IRAN ALIVE!

*Again Jesus spoke to them, saying, "I am the light of the world. Whoever follows me will not walk in darkness, but will have the light of life" (John 8:12).*

What two terrible things happened to Padina that made her want to take her life?

How did Pastor Hormoz challenge Padina?

What miracle did God do the next morning?

How did Padina and her mother become secret missionaries to their neighbors?

## CHAPTER 16 – A MAN ON A DONKEY

*[Jesus said,] "Come to me, all who labor and are heavy laden, and I will give you rest" (Matthew 11:28).*

What was so shocking to Taher at the beginning of the story? Why had this happened?

What made Taher finally lose faith in the Koran?

Describe Taher's dream. What frightened him about it?

Why were the Christians in the church frightened when they saw him?

## CHAPTER 17 – LIVING WATER IN THE DESERT

*[Jesus said,] "Whoever believes in me, as the Scripture has said, 'Out of his heart will flow rivers of living water'" (John 7:38).*

In 1979, great persecution against Christians began. But this is when Christianity started growing in Iran by large numbers. Why do you think that is?

# HIDDEN HEROES SERIES

Hidden Heroes 1: *With Two Hands:*
*True Stories of God at Work in Ethiopia*
ISBN: 978-1-84550-539-4

Hidden Heroes 2: *The Good News Must Go Out:*
*True Stories of God at Work in the Central African Republic*
ISBN: 978-1-84550-628-5

Hidden Heroes 3: *Witness Men:*
*True Stories of God at Work in Papua, Indonesia*
ISBN: 978-1-78191-515-8

Hidden Heroes 4: *Return of the White Book:*
*True Stories of God at Work in Southeast Asia*
ISBN: 978-1-78191-292-8

Hidden Heroes 5: *Lights in a Dark Place*:
*True Stories of God at Work in Colombia*
ISBN: 978-1-78191-409-0

Hidden Heroes 6: *Living Water in the Desert:*
*True Stories of God at Work in Iran*
ISBN: 978-1-78191-563-9

CHRISTIAN FOCUS PUBLICATIONS

Christian Focus | Christian Heritage | CF4K | Mentor

Christian Focus Publications publishes books for adults and children under its four main imprints: Christian Focus, CF4K, Mentor and Christian Heritage. Our books reflect our conviction that God's Word is reliable and Jesus is the way to know him, and live for ever with him.

Our children's publication list includes a Sunday School curriculum that covers pre-school to early teens, and puzzle and activity books. We also publish personal and family devotional titles, biographies and inspirational stories that children will love.

If you are looking for quality Bible teaching for children then we have an excellent range of Bible stories and age-specific theological books.

From pre-school board books to teenage apologetics, we have it covered!

**Find us at our web page:
www.christianfocus.com**

CF4•K
Because you're never
too young to know Jesus